Islamic Economics Series – 20

D0989086

Role of the State in the Economy

An Islamic Perspective

MUHAMMAD NEJATULLAH SIDDIQI

The Islamic Foundation

© The Islamic Foundation 1996/1416 AH

ISBN 0 86037 251 0 (Hb)
ISBN 0 86037 252 9 (Pb)

All rights reserved. No part of this publication may be reproduced, stored in a retrieval system, or transmitted in any form or by any means, electronic, mechanical, photocopying, recording, or otherwise, without the prior permission of the copyright owner.

Views expressed by the writer represent his personal views and do not necessarily represent the views of the Islamic Foundation.

Published by
The Islamic Foundation,
Markfield Dawah Centre,
Ratby Lane,
Markfield,
Leicester LE67 9RN,
United Kingdom

Quran House,
PO Box 30611,
Nairobi,
Kenya

PMB 3193,
Kano,
Nigeria

Printed by The Cromwell Press,
Broughton Gifford, Melksham,
Wiltshire SN12 8PH

بسم الله الرحمن الرحيم

Contents

Foreword

As the twentieth century approaches its end, economists, intellectuals and policy makers are once again grappling with the question of the role of the state in the economy – a question that has agitated their minds for at least the last two hundred years. With the sudden collapse of Socialism in the Soviet Union and Eastern Europe at the close of the last decade, there was euphoria about the 'final victory' of economic liberalism and even whispers about 'the end of history'. Privatization, both at domestic and global levels, was projected as the panacea for almost all economic ills.

This jubilation, however, proved short lived. The imperfections of the market economy, the structural problems of income and wealth distribution and of regional and global disparities, the pressing concerns for social justice, the increasing realization of the need for support and subsidy for the poor and the underprivileged, the subtle manipulations of oligopolistic, monopolistic, monopsonic and transnational corporations and cartels and the effects of open and concealed protectionistic policies of a number of developed countries have *inter alia* once again focused the attention of economists as well as policy makers on the need for some critical role for the state in the economy.

The realities of the world economy do not justify promotion of a totally neutral concept of the state. While the centralized Communist economy has failed, there is a pressing need for some kind of cooperation and co-partnership between the public and private sectors. A truly balanced market economy is possible only if the state plays a positive role to maintain those conditions which ensure smooth and harmonious working of the economy. Moreover, because of the difference in stages of growth and development and disparities in income, wealth, technology and resource endowments, justice cannot be achieved without the state and its organs playing a positive role.

The crucial questions, however, relate to the nature, extent and modes of state intervention. The tragic experiences of Socialism with all its bureaucratic mismanagement of the economy and its political misuse demand that the state should act, not primarily as an entrepreneur, but as a guide and regulator for the achievement of certain well-defined social objectives. Its role as a referee is more crucial than playing the part of a contestant.

Issues about the role of the state that are being debated amongst economists and policy makers all over the world are also being seriously discussed by Islamic economists, who have always been concerned with the middle path. Professor Dr. M. Nejatullah Siddiqi, a pioneer in the field of Islamic economics and a Faisal Laureate, has been grappling with some of these issues from his early youth. His book, *Islām kā Naẓarīyah-e-Milkīyat* (Islamic Theory of Property) appeared in the mid-sixties and has assumed the position of a classic in Islamic economic literature. He, however, has been constantly reflecting upon and reviewing the central issues of the debate and has during the last few years contributed a number of articles dealing with different dimensions of the state's role in the economy. His distinct contribution lies in discussing these issues in the context of the current economic debate as well as from an Islamic perspective. In the present work, after discussing the theoretical position of the role of the state in an Islamic economy, he has examined in depth the question of society guaranteeing a minimum level of living to all inhabitants of an Islamic state. This is followed by an essay on the question of public expenditure in an Islamic state and how to keep the monster in check. Dr. Siddiqi has also addressed himself to the question of public borrowing in early Islamic history and has come up with ample evidence to show that public borrowing for development and need fulfilment is not an altogether modern or novel phenomenon. Along with discussing the role of the state in the domestic economy, he has also tried to explore the nature and scope of its role in international economic relations. The last chapter in this study is extremely important as it brings into sharp focus the unique character of an Islamic economy where a very strong voluntary altruistic sector plays a crucial role in creating those social and economic conditions which may ensure a more effective and respectable role for the private entrepreneur and also supplement the market mechanism in establishing a just social order. It seems that Islam envisions an economy as a three-sector model – private, voluntary altruistic and public – and not merely in the groves of a public-private dichotomy. I hope the publication of this collection of essays will enable students and scholars alike to have a better understanding of the role of the state in an Islamic economy.

Leicester **Khurshid Ahmad**
10 October 1995
15 Jumāda Al-Ūlā

Preface

The State is receding from the economy, and rightly so. Seventy years of state management in the Eastern Bloc and half a century of welfarism in the West have taught some valuable lessons. Information is the key to management. But there is no way a centralized administration can get all the information at the right time. Incentives and motivation are crucial for human action. Even though they are not entirely individualistic (selfish) in nature, they do inhere in the individual. While Socialism struggled along with artificial motivation, the welfare state weakened incentives and created dependency. Change is a fact of life and adaptation to changing circumstances is necessary for progress. But state management tends to be more rigid and inflexible than private management, causing it to lose out in terms of efficiency. Last, but not least, the bigger the government the more vulnerable it is to corruption and authoritarianism thus leading to tyranny.

All that is history. At least for some time, mankind is not likely to repeat the mistake of the twentieth century: Socialism and welfarism.

But that is not the end of the state. Nothing has happened to demonstrate that justice, especially social justice can be ensured without the state playing an active role. Three centuries of capitalism have only affirmed that social justice does not obtain automatically. And the lesson to learn from the experience of the twentieth century is that we cannot get through coercion and state intervention something for which no basis exists in the individual's world view and motivation. The stronger that basis the better the results. But either way, social justice has to be administered. In performing this essential function the state may underperform or overdo. But there is no substitute for its role.

This is the subject of this book – in the Islamic perspective. It affirms the importance of the state in Islamic society and underlines its place as an active agent in the economy. Quoting the Qur'ān and the *Sunnah,* it enumerates the essential economic functions of an Islamic state and examines them in their contemporary settings. It offers no agenda for any particular Muslim country. Yet it has all of them in view when it discusses the state's responsibility towards its citizens, public expenditure, taxation, borrowing and international economic relations.

Chapter One, 'Guarantee of a Minimum Level of Living in an Islamic State', highlights the cooperative nature of Islamic living by making the bold statement that 'The Constitution of an Islamic State must contain a clause guaranteeing the fulfilment of basic needs to every human being within its territorial jurisdiction.'

Chapter Two, 'Public Expenditure in an Islamic State', follows up by focusing on other related functions. It examines the possibility of enlarging the area of state activity in the economy, should circumstances so require.

Chapter Three, 'Public Borrowing in Early Islamic History', conveys the message that responsible borrowing has a place in the quest for need fulfilment and economic development.

Chapter Four, 'International Economic Relations in Islam', introduces an essential but somewhat neglected dimension of state activity, that relating to the rest of humanity, especially the world Islamic community.

Chapter Five, 'Role of the Voluntary Sector in Islam', serves as a reminder that the state and the individual are not the only players. The voluntary sector also has a significant role.

Since the Islamic state has a significant role in ensuring social justice and nudging economic activity towards spiritual-moral goals, it must pay special attention to the four issues noted above: information, incentives, adaptability to change, and vulnerability to authoritarianism and corruption.

Collection and dissemination of information can be given top priority. Besides spiritual and moral orientation, incentives can be provided to encourage socially-oriented behaviour. Decentralization and local autonomy can increase flexibility. Politics should be so conducted as to propel the honest to a decision-making position and discredit the dishonest before they become too strong. A system of checks and balances has to be devised to keep authority accountable and restrained. Rather than swinging between the experience of individualism bordering on anarchy and collective organization stifling freedom and initiative, the spirit of Islam calls for keeping to the middle path.

An expanding role for the state may involve some trade off. A gain in justice and equity is worth some loss in efficiency. As regards corruption and tyranny, they are antithetical to Islam. They are entirely unacceptable. No progress is worth tyranny. So the question arises: What are we going to do about big government's tendency to become corrupt and tyrannical?

The first thing is to internalize moral values so that economic agents are well behaved and the need for state intervention is minimized. Let the individual be oriented towards socially-responsible behaviour through education. This will automatically lead to the second step: enlarging the voluntary sector so that it does some of the jobs big government has appropriated. The third step is political. A system of representative government where rulers are accountable to the people and individuals have the freedom to observe, express their views and associate with one another.

All three are essential parts of Islamic living. Unfortunately, whereas in practice the first two have fared tolerably well, the third has fared badly. There are many good Muslims and many voluntary activities but little representative government, even less accountability, and rarely the essential freedoms in the Muslim political structures of today.

Those who read this volume to get an idea about Islamic economic management in the contemporary setting should keep these facts in mind. The active role of the state envisaged in this study presumes representative government accountable to a people who enjoy basic freedoms. To ensure this is no less important than internalization of the Islamic moral values emphasized above.

There are no short cuts.

Essays included in this volume were first published as under:

* 'Guarantee of a Minimum Level of Living in an Islamic State' in *Distributive Justice and Need Fulfilment in an Islamic Economy,* ed. Munawar Iqbal (Leicester, The Islamic Foundation, 1988), pp. 251–86.

* 'Public Expenditure in an Islamic State' in *Economic Journal,* Govt. College, Lahore, Vol. XIX, Nos. 1–2 (1986). But this text taken from *Development and Finance in Islam,* ed. A.H.M. Sadeq, A.H. Pramanik, N.M.b.H. Hasan (Malaysia, International Islamic University, 1991).

* 'An Overview of Public Borrowing in Early Islamic History', *Review of Islamic Economics,* Vol. 2, No. 2 (1993), pp 1–16.

* 'Principles of International Economic Relations in Islam' in *International Economic Relations From Islamic Perspective* (IRTI, Jeddah, Islamic Development Bank, 1992), pp. 9–34.

* 'Role of the Voluntary Sector in Islam: A Conceptual Framework' in *The Islamic Voluntary Sector in South East Asia* (Singapore, Institute of South East Asian Studies, 1991), pp. 6–30.

Jeddah
July 1995
Safar 1416 AH

Muhammad Nejatullah Siddiqi

CHAPTER ONE

Guarantee of a Minimum Level of Living in an Islamic State

Introduction

The vision of an organized Islamic living that inspires the Muslims today has some important dimensions that have not been studied properly. One of these is a guarantee of fulfilment of the basic needs of everyone. This, seen in the context of the Islamic view of life on earth, the nature of the relationship between man and man in Islam, and the function of society and its basic institutions such as the family and the state, is a very important principle. Since it emanates from the core of the Islamic view of life which is essentially spiritual and ethical, it occupies a higher place in the order of priorities than a similar proposition of a modern welfare state conceived at the material level and operating in the framework of expediency and pragmatism.

This chapter seeks to study this principle, and addresses such questions as:

- What is the nature of this guarantee?
- What is its basis in the *Sharī'ah*?
- How does it relate to the Islamic view of life and where does it stand in the hierarchy of Islamic values?
- What are those needs whose fulfilment is guaranteed?
- Who are those responsible for fulfilling this guarantee?
- What are the ways and means for meeting this obligation?

What are its operational implications in the contemporary situation?

Nature of the Guarantee

A word on the nature of this guarantee is necessary at the outset to clear up any possible misunderstanding. It is *not* asserted that a basketful of life's necessaries would be doled out to every individual in all circumstances. Individuals are normally expected to fulfil their needs through their own efforts. Since this is ingrained in human nature the *Sharī'ah* does not proclaim it emphatically. But the *Sharī'ah* does lay down very explicitly that preservation of one's life is a duty.[1] One is not allowed to starve oneself to death or kill oneself by voluntarily depriving oneself of any of the other necessaries such as clothing, shelter, etc.[2] The *Sharī'ah* requires every individual to strive for the fulfilment of life's basic needs. Living does not, however, mean bare physical survival. What is desired is living for a purpose. This requires living with efficiency and dignity so that the individual is enabled to pursue his purpose.

This guarantee applies to everyone, irrespective of age, sex, race, colour, language, caste or creed. It applies to Muslims as well as non-Muslims. The only criterion for eligibility is need, without sufficient means to fulfil it. Some members of society are permanently placed in this category because of some debility, e.g. the invalid, the blind and the chronically ill, the very old and the very young, etc. Some are temporarily found in this condition, such as the unemployed and those with insufficient incomes. These types of people are guaranteed fulfilment of their basic needs through a number of direct and indirect means. It is this guarantee which is the subject of this study.

Basis in the *Sharī'ah*

The guarantee of need fulfilment or the right to a livelihood follows logically from the Islamic view of life. It is inferred from some texts in the Qur'ān. Certain traditions from the Prophet state it clearly, while others imply it. The Rightly-

Guided Caliphs recognized it to be one of their responsibilities and acted accordingly. Lastly, the principle is upheld in the juridical literature and affirmed by eminent Islamic thinkers, past and present. We shall elaborate these points below. Though the principle is generally recognized, it is necessary to cite the relevant verses, traditions and precedents as these are not easily accessible to all.

The right to a livelihood follows from the Islamic view of life as a test, the status of men and women as vicegerents, and their being distinguished from other creatures by a special dignity; from the fact that the universe has been well provisioned to sustain human life; and from the cooperative nature of the Islamic society.

1. Life on earth is a test:

> Blessed is He in Whose hand is the Sovereignty and He is Able to do all things. Who has created life and death that He may try you, which of you is best in conduct, and He is the Mighty, the Forgiving (67: 1, 2).

A test requires the capacity to be subjected to that test. The person whose conduct is to be scrutinized must be living and life requires the fulfilment of needs. It follows that in order for the purpose of creation to be realized, the basic needs of humans should be fulfilled. Since a test is meaningful only when one is freely able to choose between alternatives, need fulfilment should go beyond ensuring physical survival to facilitating an efficient life.

2. Humans are the vicegerents of God on earth[3] which means they have specific functions to perform. This presumes that survival as well as efficiency have to be ensured.

The Prophet is reported to have emphasized the same point by saying: 'The world is green and sweet and Allah would put it under your charge and see how you behave.'[4]

The Qur'ān declares human beings to be dignified and dignity presumes need fulfilment whereas deprivation is contrary to it.

> Verily We have honoured the children of Adam. We carry them on land and the sea and have made provision of good things for them, and have preferred them above many of those whom We created with a marked preferment (17: 70).

3. Several verses of the Qur'ān affirm that sufficient provisions have been made in man's environment with the specific purpose that he should avail himself of these and so have his needs fulfilled.[5]

> And We have given you (mankind) power in the earth, and appointed for you therein a livelihood. Little give you thanks! (7: 10).

The fact that provisions provided by the Creator are sufficient for all, coupled with His desire that everyone should draw his sustenance from these provisions, make it a socially-obligatory duty (*farḍ kifāyah*) to ensure need fulfilment for such members of society as cannot obtain it for themselves. This point is further elaborated below (12).

4. Traditions from the Prophet declare a state of deprivation to be undesirable and something which is to be eliminated. These traditions and some verses of the Qur'ān recognize such a state as the basis for entitlement to a provision. Lastly, they make the society and its rulers responsible for looking after the needy and arranging for the fulfilment of their needs.

The Prophet prayed: 'Allah, I ask Thy refuge from apostasy and poverty', whereupon a person enquired, 'Are the two similar?' The Prophet said: 'Yes.'[6] He also advised: 'Seek Allah's refuge from poverty, scarcity and ignominy.'[7]

Primarily, it is one's own duty to earn a livelihood. The Prophet said: 'To earn an honest livelihood is a duty (ranking) next to the chief duty (of offering prayers).'[8]

5. Islam regards mankind as a brotherhood in which the natural relationship between human beings is that of cooperation. The Prophet is reported to have said: 'I am witness to the fact that all servants (of Allah) are brethren',[9] and he urged all to live accordingly: 'O, servants of Allah, live as brethren (of one another).'[10] The Qur'ān emphasizes cooperation:

> . . . help you one another unto righteousness and pious duty . . . (5: 2).

and declares this to be the normal relationship between believers:

> And the believers, men and women, are protecting friends one of another . . . (9: 71).[11]

It is unimaginable that the needy should go uncared for in such a collectivity of brethren and protecting friends. The Qur'ān ascribes denial of this obligation to support the needy to the disbelievers, clearly implying that the believers must recognize this obligation and live up to it.[12]

6. That a state of poverty and deprivation entitles one to social support is a principle recognized by the Qur'ān and the *Sunnah* sometimes by implication, as in the Qur'ānic verses:

> And in whose wealth there is a right acknowledged for the beggar and the destitute (70: 24, 25).

and sometimes directly as in the following traditions:

It is narrated that Ibn 'Umar said that the Prophet said:

> . . . a locality in which one has to starve a night is deprived of Allah's protection.[13]

It is narrated that 'Alī said that the Prophet said:

> Allah has levied upon the rich among Muslims, in their wealth, an amount that would suffice for the poor amongst them. If the poor starve or go unclad it is because of what their rich are doing. Beware, Allah the mighty and the exalted will take a tough account from them and punish them with a painful punishment.[14]

Another tradition from the Prophet says:

> Allah revealed to Mūsā son of 'Imrān . . . I have not deprived the poor because My treasure could not afford it and My mercy could not accommodate them. But I have

appointed for the poor in the wealth of the rich what would suffice for them. I decided to test the rich (and see) how they behave in respect of what I have levied upon their wealth for the poor . . .[15]

It is narrated from Ibn 'Umar that the Prophet said:

Protect one who seeks your protection in the name of Allah and give to him who asks (for something) in the name of Allah.[16]

7. The following verses of the Qur'ān also recognize poverty as a basis for the entitlement to financial support from a variety of sources from which the well-to-do are not to receive anything (i.e. *fay'*,[17] *zakāh,* and property of an orphan under one's guardianship):

That which Allah gives as spoil unto His Messenger from the people of the townships, it is for Allah and His messenger and for the near of kin and the orphans and the needy and the wayfarer, that it become not a commodity between the rich among you . . . And (it is) for the poor fugitives who have been driven out from their homes and their belongings . . . (59: 7, 8).

The alms are only for the poor and the needy, and those who collect them, and those whose hearts are to be reconciled, and to free the captives and the debtors, and for the cause of Allah, and (for) the wayfarers, a duty imposed by Allah. Allah is the knower, wise (9: 60).

Judge orphans till they reach the marriage age, then if you find them of sound judgement, deliver unto them their fortune, and devour it not by squandering and in haste lest they should grow up. Whoso (of the guardians) is rich, let him abstain generously (from taking of the property of orphans); and whoso is poor let him take thereof in reason (for his guardianship) . . . (4: 6).

8. The issue was confirmed by the Prophet, in consonance with the intention of the Qur'ānic verses cited above, by laying down the principle that the rulers bear the ultimate

responsibility for arranging the fulfilment of basic needs. The Prophet is reported to have said:

> Allah and His messenger are the guardians of one who has no guardian.[18]
>
> The ruler is the guardian of one who has no guardian.[19]
>
> One who leaves behind wealth, (the wealth) is for his family, and I am responsible for the stranded dependants (one leaves behind).[20]
>
> One whom Allah the mighty, the exalted, puts in charge of some of the affairs of the Muslims and he turns his back on their needs and necessities and poverty Allah will turn His back on his needs and necessities and poverty.[21]

9. Precedents from the Rightly-Guided Caliphs confirm this principle. These rulers were conscious of their obligations towards the needy and took measures to fulfil their needs.

'Umar publicly declared that Allah had charged him with the responsibility of preventing supplications to Him.[22] An eminent jurist explaining this statement observes that the ruler has to fulfil the needs of the people so that they are not obliged to pray to Allah for the fulfilment of their needs.[23] On another occasion 'Umar declared:

> I am keen to fulfil a need whenever I see one, as long as we are collectively capable of doing so. When we can no longer afford it we cooperate in living till everyone is living at the same level of subsistence.[24]

In fact he made it known to everyone that he could always be approached by those who needed financial support:

> Whosoever wants to ask me for money should come to me because Allah has appointed me the keeper of (His) treasury and the disbursor.[25]

He was so keenly conscious of this obligation that he thought it applicable to animals: 'If a camel dies unattended on the bank of the Euphrates, I am afraid Allah would make me accountable for it.'[26]

'Umar bin 'Abd al-'Azīz was once found weeping, and was asked what worried him; he replied: 'I have taken charge of the affairs of the community of Muḥammad, so I am worried about the hungry, poor, the unattended sick, the warrior (in the cause of Allah) the oppressed, the prisoner in alien lands, the very old, those with many dependants but little money, and similar people . . . '[27] He too had publicly declared: 'I will try my best to fulfil the need of any one of you to the extent possible if it comes to my notice.'[28]

10. Juristic opinion affirms the principle of need fulfilment and the guarantee of a minimum level of living at two levels. Firstly, jurists consider the protection of life to be one of the objectives of *Sharī'ah* along with the protection of religion. The former implies this guarantee directly and the latter indirectly. Secondly, they include need fulfilment in socially-obligatory duties (*farḍ kifāyah*).

Al-Ghazālī notes that 'the objectives of *Sharī'ah* that relate to people are five; that is to protect their religion, life, reason, progeny and property.'[29] Al-Shāṭibī observes that 'the divine law is designed to protect five basic things. These are religion, life, progeny, property and reason.'[30] Al-Ghazālī has rightly noted that religion can be preserved only through acquiring knowledge and offering prayers, both of which presume 'bodily health, survival and availability of a minimum of clothing, housing, and other supplies.'[31] Hence, the protection of religion also necessitates need fulfilment, which is already a must for ensuring another objective of *Sharī'ah,* i.e. the protection of life.

11. Jurists include fulfilling the needs of the destitute in the list of socially-obligatory duties (*farḍ kifāyah*). The nature of these duties has been explained by al-Shāṭibī as follows:

> Their being socially obligatory means that their performance is not the duty of any particular individual. They devolve on the totality of all individuals, so that those common interests are protected without which individual interests cannot be safe. They reinforce and complement the aforementioned (individually necessary objectives of the *Sharī'ah*), hence these are also necessary. Individual

> objectives cannot be realized without the social ones. Social objectives relate to the good of all men . . . They aim at preserving human life. Individuals are the vicegerents of Allah amidst servants of Allah, to the extent allowed by their abilities and powers. But a single individual has hardly the ability to set his own affairs right, not to mention the affairs of his family, kinsfolk, tribe, or the humanity at large. That is why Allah has entrusted the fulfilment of common needs of mankind to society as a whole. That is the *raison d'être* of the state in society.[32]

According to al-Nawawī, socially-obligatory duties include the 'elimination of suffering by providing clothes to the unclad, food to the hungry . . .'[33]

Ibn Ḥazm is more specific on this issue:

> It is the duty of the rich in every country to support the poor. If the revenue from *Zakāh* and the *fay'* of all Muslims does not suffice for this purpose, the ruler will oblige them to fulfil their responsibility. Enough funds will be mobilized for these (needy people) to provide them with food, clothing for summer and winter, and a house that protects them from rain, heat and sun and gives them privacy.[34]

As implied by al-Shāṭibī in the text quoted above, the ultimate responsibility for assisting the needy in the context of socially-obligatory duties rests with the rulers. Al-Ghazālī, therefore, lays down very clearly that:

> It is incumbent on the ruler to help the people when they are facing scarcity, starving and suffering especially during a famine or when prices are high. People fail to earn a living in these circumstances and it becomes difficult for them to make both ends meet. The rulers should, in these circumstances, feed the people and give them financial assistance from their treasury in order to improve their lot.[35]

The eminent Ḥanafī jurist, al-Jaṣṣāṣ, makes the same point in his commentary on *Sūrah Yūsuf* in the Qur'ān.[36] The same opinion has been expressed by al-Sarakhsī who has quoted Imām Muḥammad bin Ḥasan al-Shaybānī in his support.[37]

12. There is a consensus of contemporary writers on this principle. Mawdūdī, Sayyid Quṭb, Muṣṭafā al-Sibā'ī, Muḥammad Abū Zahrah, Muḥammad Bāqir al-Ṣadr, Muḥammad al-Mubārak and Yūsuf al-Qaraḍāwī have all affirmed the principle that every human being within the territorial limits of an Islamic state is to be guaranteed a minimum level of living and that the ultimate responsibility in this regard lies with the Islamic state.[38]

To sum up the arguments of this section, the principle that the basic needs of every human being must be fulfilled, is fully established in the *Sharī'ah.* The individual himself, his near relatives, the neighbourhood, and the society must all recognize and fulfil their responsibilities in this regard. But the ultimate responsibility of implementing this principle in practice rests with the Islamic state. It is part of the Islamic vision. It is implied in the Islamic view of life by the status of human beings on earth and the cooperative nature of the Islamic society. It is supported by the texts of the Qur'ān and the *Sunnah* and by the Caliphal precedents. It finds unanimous endorsement by past jurists and more recent writers on Islam who have discussed this issue.

Significance of the Principle

Before we proceed to examine what needs are covered by this principle, it is advisable to note its special significance. Firstly, even though the object of the guarantee is certain material provisions, its basis is religious. It is part of Islam's religious view of life and its neglect will distort that view. It is an important objective of *Sharī'ah,* and its non-implementation will defeat the overall purpose of *Sharī'ah.* It is part of the religious duties in Islam, and the individuals to whom this duty relates neglect it only at their peril in the Hereafter. The principle is intrinsic to the nature of Islamic society and its neglect will disrupt its social fabric. It is basic to the concept of the state in Islam and belongs to the core of its functions. In view of the religious nature of this principle, it can neither be abrogated nor suspended under any circumstances. Man simply does not have the authority to do so, once the divine nature of the principle is established. It is not predicated by any conditions pertaining to a particular stage of economic development by a society or the details of its political structure.

Secondly, the principle ranks highly in the objectives of *Sharī'ah,* because it relates to the survival of the individual. The objectives relating to the protection of one's religion, property, progeny or reason are meaningful and relevant only if one survives so as to function. It follows that the realization of any other objective of *Sharī'ah* presupposes the implementation of this principle. This necessitates that this principle be at the top of the agenda for any Islamic activity or movement, and especially for the Islamic state. There would be something basically wrong with a state or movement which does not recognize this priority. A failure to do so cannot emanate from strategic considerations, its cause is a misconception about Islam itself.

Needs to be Fulfilled

1. Once the principle is established, those needs which have to be fulfilled can be identified easily. There can be no doubt that food, clothing and shelter (i.e. housing) are necessary for bare survival. They are included in the list of every writer who has discussed the subject. Depending on climatic conditions and social circumstances, drinking water, fuel and electricity would also be part of this package. Medical care in case of illness, some education for the illiterate and general Islamic instruction for all Muslims, are also regarded as basic needs. One can add transport, especially in big cities. The blind and the invalid need attendance without which they can hardly survive. Some writers have also included such needs as the financial support needed to get married. Financial assistance to repay debts, aid to buy necessary trade tools and even the provision of some facilities for recreation also find mention in some studies.[39] The basis of all these additions in the list is what constitutes necessary provision to ensure survival with efficiency and dignity. Reference is possible to some traditions from the Prophet as well as to precedents from the Rightly-Guided

Caliphs on some of these points. Leaving aside the need for food, clothing, shelter and medical care, the case for which is obvious and derives unambiguously from the principle, we shall note below the precedents supporting the case of other needs.

2. Traditions from the Prophet say that he used to send instructors to teach people the tenets of religion as well as reading and writing.[40] He had appointed Sa'īd bin al-'Āṣ to teach people in Madīnah to read and write.[41] 'Umar appointed teachers for the children in Madīnah.[42] Similarly, 'Umar bin 'Abd al-'Azīz appointed salaried instructors for people in the village.[43] Stipends were given by him to students and those engaged in academic pursuits.[44]

There are precedents from 'Umar bin al-Khaṭṭāb[45] as well as 'Umar bin 'Abd al-'Azīz[46] for supplying attendants to the blind and the invalid, etc. 'Umar is also reported to have provided transport for the needy,[47] and 'Umar bin 'Abd al-'Azīz gave financial grants for marriage.[48]

As we have argued above, these precedents only serve to strengthen a case already established. For, 'what is necessary to do in order to perform an obligatory duty itself becomes an obligatory duty.'[49] Once we establish the principle that protection and the preservation of human life through need fulfilment is a duty, it becomes a duty to fulfil any need that is recognized as necessary for survival. The case for food, clothing, shelter, child care, medical care for the sick, attendance for the blind and the invalid and transportation for the stranded is obvious in this context. Al-Ramlī states that: 'It is necessary to provide clothing that covers the whole of the body and is adequate for summer and winter. With food and drink are included expenses which are equally necessary such as doctor's fees, cost of medicine and attendants for the invalid, as is obvious.'[50]

The case for literacy and Islamic instruction derives from the efficiency and the protection of religion. Depending on the circumstances, other needs can also be added to this list.

3. To what extent a particular need should be fulfilled is again a matter in which, besides the requirements of survival

with efficiency and dignity, the economic conditions of a society play a decisive role. A standard of need fulfilment cannot be set without reference to the average standard of living in a country. Things which may be easily dispensed with in one country may be necessary for an efficient and dignified living in another country. Life would be very hard without a refrigerator in New York, though it is not indispensable in Delhi. Another factor that would have a decisive influence in setting a standard is the economic resources of the country concerned. If a country is poor and no great surpluses are available in the society, the standard aimed at will be defined more by the requirements of survival with reasonable efficiency than by the average standard of living in the society. But if a country is rich and the revenue from *zakāh* and *fay'* itself can provide the fulfilment of these needs to an extent that brings the level of living of the needy closer to the average level of living in the society, it should aim at these standards. Should it be necessary to tax further, and surpluses be available with the rich in society, the same standards, i.e. not far below the social average, are recommended. Like other important issues in the polity of Islam, these details are to be decided through a process of consultation (*shūrā*). The democratic procedure is expected to throw up decisions that are both realistic as well as satisfactory to all concerned. But the principle has to be implemented whatever the standard of living. Even when the total resources are meagre, provision for everyone has to be made to ensure survival if not sufficiency. It is perhaps needless to emphasize that such a situation calls for a constant endeavour to develop and produce more. The following quotations support our argument:

> It is reported by Abū Mūsā al-Ash'arī that the Prophet said: 'When the Ash'arīs face scarcity during *Jihād* or are short of food in Madīnah they collect whatever they have on one sheet of cloth and then distribute it equally among themselves by the same measure. Hence they are mine and I am one of them.'[51]

> It is reported of Jābir bin 'Abdullāh that he said that the Prophet sent a party towards the coast. They were three hundred in number and he appointed Abū 'Ubaydah bin

> al-Jarrāḥ as their commander. I was one of them. We set off but we had gone only part of the way when our provisions fell short. Abū 'Ubaydah then ordered collection of provisions from the whole army and everything was collected. The entire collection was two bags of dates. He gave us a little every day, till this too was exhausted and we were receiving only one date . . .[52]
>
> It is reported of Jābir bin 'Abdullāh that he said that the Prophet said: 'O Muhājirīn and Anṣār, there are some amongst your brethren who have neither wealth nor kinsmen so each one of you should admit two or three of them (for supporting them)'.[53]

A policy statement made by 'Umar during the year of famine in Madīnah is very revealing:

> It is reported by Ibn 'Umar that 'Umar said: 'If I had no money to fulfil the need of the people and the only way left (to fulfil their needs) was to make every household share their provisions with an equal number, everyone being only half fed, till Allah gave us rain, I would have done so. For men can still survive on half the food they need.'[54]

These precedents clearly indicate that the guarantee of a minimum level of living must be available to every individual, even though this minimum has to be decided in accordance with the actual conditions. It may be very low in extremely bad circumstances when there are no surpluses to be mobilized. But in normal conditions it is defined with reference to the average standard of living in a society.

Ways and Means of Need Fulfilment

1. The above discussion has already taken care of the question as to who is responsible for fulfilling the needs of the people. Since it is characterized as *farḍ kifāyah* (a socially-obligatory duty), the voluntary action of well-to-do individuals is expected to play a substantial role in this connection. Besides individual action we can envisage an active role on the part of associations and organizations. The institution of charitable

endowments or *awqāf* in Islam is a typical example of how private initiative may result in semi-public arrangements for need fulfilment.

As we have argued above, the ultimate responsibility for need fulfilment rests with the state. Traditions from the Prophet and the Caliphal precedents quoted above confirm this view. As we have seen above, the state is ultimately responsible for all socially-obligatory duties, and need fulfilment is a socially-obligatory duty. There is unanimity on this point among contemporary writers on Islam who have discussed this issue. What needs to be explored further is the proper way and means of doing so in the modern context. The available precedents pertain to an entirely different set of conditions. The increase in the population, the development of transport and communications, the advance of technology, the multiplication of administrative facilities and the existence of a variety of social organizations have opened up new possibilities and at the same time have enlarged the dimensions of the task itself.

2. The first source of an individual's need fulfilment is his own income. He is normally expected to provide for himself and his wife and children by earning through services currently rendered and/or out of income from assets inherited or acquired in the past. A large number of individuals in any contemporary society have, however, neither income nor assets. Most of these are able to work and are willing to do so, but they cannot find a job. There is yet a larger group whose income (from both sources) is less than sufficient. Though the immediate objective of the guarantee is to extend assistance to them, in cash or kind, to fulfil their needs, the long-run objective should be to help them acquire remunerative jobs so that they can fulfil their needs on their own. This policy has some precedents in the *Sunnah*.[55]

3. The next source of need fulfilment for a person is support from his near relatives. In certain cases this obligation is legal. The husband has to provide for his wife irrespective of his or her financial condition. Next come one's parents and children. One's obligation towards them, however, depends on one being financially capable of doing so. A person with sufficient means

is obliged to provide for his needy parents, needy offspring as long as they are minors, and for such adult offspring as are incapable of providing for themselves because of sickness or debility. Thus far, all schools of Islamic law are unanimous.[56] Opinions differ regarding one's entitlement to obligatory support from other relatives. According to Aḥmad bin Ḥanbal, an individual with means is obliged to support any needy relative from whom he might inherit upon his death.[57] For other opinions and the relevant details a reference to proper sources is advisable. For our purpose it is sufficient to point out the role these obligations are likely to play in the context of the guarantee that is the subject of this study. Social pressure as well as the courts would ensure that this role is carried out effectively.

4. Private charity and support from philanthropic organizations and voluntary associations can also be a substantial source of support for the needy. It has been especially so in the Islamic society. But person-to-person help is incapable of playing as effective a role in the modern industrial society, especially in the urban metropolis, as it used to do because of the lack of direct contact and communication between individuals. It is much easier and far more effective for those willing to help, to operate through an association or social agency than to personally locate the needy and take care of their needs. For the needy too it is easier to approach institutions rather than individuals. There will always be some scope for person-to-person support, but more reliance has to be placed on institutions. Assuming that the *zakāh* of the apparent wealth (e.g. cattle, crops and merchandise) will be collected by the state, and part of the *zakāh* on non-apparent wealth (e.g. cash holdings and bullion) may also be mobilized by it, the obvious sources of funds for these institutions are voluntary *zakāh* payment on non-apparent wealth, general charity and revenue from endowments. It is difficult to specify what forms these institutions will take. One can refer to the forms prevalent in the Muslim society like orphanages, free hospitals, free educational institutions, guest-houses for the wayfarer, etc. One can also borrow from the contemporary charitable institutions, especially in the West which play a major role in the areas of health and

education, and care for the invalid, the very old and the very young.

5. There are some temporary or accidental needs for which an individual with means can provide in advance. For example, an individual can provide for his old age by saving part of his income during his working life, or can protect himself against accidents resulting in a loss of income-earning capacity through insurance. Since the individuals' failure to do so would increase the burden on the Social Authority and its need fulfilment programmes, it should step in to make the necessary arrangements. Thus, a state-administered scheme of social insurance can take care of old age, temporary unemployment, sickness, industrial accidents and similar eventualities. Financially-capable individuals should be obliged to make suitable contributions out of their earnings so that they are assured of adequate support when it is needed. Medical care in the case of sickness can also be supplied on the same basis. In order to cover those who are not in a position to make any contributions, either because they are not earning or because their incomes are very low, the state has to make contributions over and above those it can mobilize from the financially-capable beneficiaries. It is important to remember this point as we proceed to examine the sources of funds for a state-administered comprehensive programme of need fulfilment.

6. As noted above, the ultimate responsibility for need fulfilment rests with the Islamic state. Should a needy individual fail to find support from his near relatives and other private sources, the state is obliged to come to his assistance.

The different ways in which the state can do so are discussed in the next section. Before taking up that discussion, let us look at the sources of funds required to finance such a state programme. The source funds for a state-administered social security programme are revenue from *zakāh,* and other state revenue and taxes levied especially for this purpose. In principle, a recourse to the last source is called for only when the first two means do not suffice for the purpose.

That the major object of *zakāh* revenue is need fulfilment is a point which need not be argued here as sufficient literature is already available on this subject.[58] Some appropriation from general state revenue is justified on the ground that this revenue would normally include *fay'*, which has to be used for this purpose in case *zakāh* revenue does not suffice. This has been stressed by several jurists quoted above. The only point that needs substantiation is the right of the Islamic state to tax the rich for this purpose. These are taxes over and above those provided in the *Sharī'ah,* e.g. *zakāh,* and distinct from those necessitated by the society's mandate to the state to maintain civil amenities and public utilities. The case has been stated well by Ibn Ḥazm as already noted: 'It is the duty of the rich in every country to support the poor. If the revenue from *zakāh* and the *fay'* of all Muslims does not suffice for this purpose, the ruler will oblige them to fulfil their responsibility. Enough funds will be mobilized for these (needy people) to provide them with food, clothing for summer and winter, and a house that protects them from rain, heat and sun and gives them privacy.'[59]

This is, in principle, the stand emerging from Islamic jurisprudence. In fact, our argument in the earlier sections inevitably leads to the conclusion that the Islamic state has a right to tax the rich to ensure need fulfilment, should normal sources of revenue not suffice for this purpose. The reason we do not find very explicit texts on this issue in the early compendia of Islamic law is because such a situation rarely obtained in that period, the normal revenue of the public treasury being sufficient for this purpose. Whenever the need for additional taxation did arise, jurists came forth to affirm this right. Apart from the above text from Ibn Ḥazm, we have the opinion of al-Shāṭibī,[60] al-Ghazālī,[61] 'Izuddīn bin 'Abd al-Salām,[62] al-Māwardī,[63] Abū Ya'lā,[64] the Mālikī jurist al-Bājī,[65] and the Ḥanafī jurists al-Sarakhsī[66] and al-Qurṭubī,[67] affirming the state's right to levy additional taxes in certain circumstances.

7. Before concluding this section on the ways and means of ensuring need fulfilment, it is important to note that in the long run it requires increased production and an ensured economic growth. To divert part of a rising GNP to the poor is easier and less painful than doing so out of a given total income. The

programme of need fulfilment should be conceived as part of a dynamic process of growth and redistribution in which a more equitable distribution contributes to growth by raising the productivity of labour and so higher levels of GNP facilitate a more equitable distribution.

Contemporary Policy Implications

1. How should a modern Islamic state handle this issue? No less important than the actual implementation of the guarantee is a clear declaration of intent. The constitution of an Islamic state must contain a clause incorporating this principle. This is needed to reassure the weak and the poor that the state stands by them as well as to ensure that no government fails in its duty. In fact, the clause should be justiciable so that any citizen, not necessarily those affected, could go to court to secure the implementation of this principle.[68] There must be a way for the one actually in need of food, clothing and shelter, etc. necessary for survival, to get his need fulfilled through some social agency which is easily accessible. No other conditions should be attached to this facility except the actual need. While the help-seeker may subsequently be obliged to work if he can, the fact of being in need of food, clothing, shelter or medical care should be sufficient to entitle him to support from the appropriate state agency.

2. Before we consider some policies likely to ensure universal need fulfilment we note three principles that will guide us in this discussion. Firstly, there should be the least interference with the market process which results in the pricing of commodities and factors, allocates resources and distributes the product. Secondly, the long-run objective should be to enable the needy to acquire the necessary means to fulfil their needs on their own, making social grants unnecessary. Lastly, it is imperative that the objective of need fulfilment is realized in the short run as well as in the long run, whatever the extent of the interference with the market process it may involve. Under no circumstances is this objective to be sacrificed for other goals such as growth or freedom. The degree of need fulfilment and the standard of living that is actually guaranteed to the poor in

the short run is, however, to be determined by taking these goals into consideration, especially the requirements of long-run growth on which future improvements in this standard also depend.

We shall indicate below some policies suitable for ensuring need fulfilment in the contemporary situation. In doing so, we draw upon Islamic traditions as well as contemporary experience. The list is by no means exhaustive. Any other policy that serves the end and fits into the framework of Islamic values can be included in the package.

3. *Direct Transfer of Income to the Poor*

The direct transfer of income to the poor is a well established policy in the Islamic tradition. It came into effect with the introduction of the obligatory *zakāh* levy in the second year after *Hijrah*[69] in the Islamic state of Madīnah. In the short run, this method is preferable to some of the other methods discussed below as it involves the least interference with the market process, hence its allocative effects are minimal.

Assuming that the income transferred to the poor comes out of taxes levied on the rich, resources will be redirected from what the rich would have demanded, had there been no taxes, to what the poor would demand, as they receive this income. Resources may, therefore, be redirected from the production of luxuries and comforts to that of necessities. This is definitely desirable.

Taxes would also cut into the savings of the rich, reducing the social surplus available for investment and capital formation. On the other hand, the productivity of labour would be expected to rise both in industry and agriculture as universal need fulfilment results in better health, improved education, etc. A sound policy package would, however, have to keep an eye on long-term investment, especially in present-day underdeveloped Muslim countries.

The least that a contemporary Islamic state must do is to levy *zakāh* and use its yield to finance its income transfers programme. Should this yield fall short of the need, additional taxes have to be levied, as noted above. It is difficult, in the absence of any empirical studies, to decide whether and to what extent this would be needed in present-day Muslim countries.

One tends to suspect, however, that in most of the poor Muslim countries additional taxation would be needed to finance a programme of universal need fulfilment. A few points in relation to such taxation are, therefore, in order.

It is imperative that additional taxation should not hit the poor. Indirect taxes would not, therefore, qualify for this purpose except when they relate to luxury items of consumption. Two obvious targets for additional direct taxation are capital gains and economic rents.[70] Such taxation does not have any disincentive effect. The taxation of these incomes does not affect the behaviour of those taxed. Besides the justification provided by social need, the taxation of capital gains and economic rents is also justified by the fact that the causes giving rise to these incomes are mostly social. Generally speaking, the efforts of those individuals who receive these incomes play a minor role.

An income transfers programme should focus, in the first instance, on the old, the blind, the chronically ill and the invalid, widows and other women without support, and children belonging to poor families. Coupled with a social insurance programme mobilizing contributions from those who can pay, the coverage of this programme can be broadened to cover all families. We can then add to this the temporarily unemployed, the victims of industrial accidents, the self employed with insufficient incomes and those whom the market considers to be unemployable. People in all these categories may be covered by the income transfers programme subject to the proviso that they are not already covered by the obligatory support from their relatives as explained above, or by any other social arrangement. Since the number of people in these categories may be substantial, amounting to about half of the total population of a country in certain cases,[71] such a programme could only be implemented in phases. It is also necessary to consider how far some of the other methods discussed below can relieve the income transfers programme of its burden.

One important issue that deserves consideration in this context is that of the effect of an income transfers programme on the incentive to work. It is argued that when need brings income, the needy may not feel obliged to work in order to earn their living. Worse still, some who are working may stop doing so and enter the category of the needy. If this is allowed to go on, production may decline, surpluses that can be mobilized through taxation may dwindle, while the needed income transfers may grow – a situation which is impossible to handle. This nightmare is, however, the result of exaggeration. To begin with, the quantum of assistance available under the programme of income transfers is not sufficient to cover all the needs of a person, hence the incentive to work and earn more would still be there. It has been rightly observed that '. . . dynamic aspects of raised consumption goals after higher income is attained may stimulate work effort in a drive for higher income.'[72] Moreover, 'research does not support the view that modest income guarantees have a serious negative effect on work motives'.[73]

4. *Public Provision of Consumption Goods and Services*

Public provision of essential consumption goods and services is a more efficient method of need fulfilment than income transfers, at least in certain circumstances. The case has been argued well by advocates of the 'basic needs' approach.[74] Consumers are not always efficient optimizers, especially as regards nutrition and health. Sometimes they spend their meagre income on items dictated by customs and rituals to the neglect of food and other essential needs. Some basic needs such as health, education, safe water and sewerage cannot be met efficiently by private purchases.[75] Furthermore, money spent by the poor generally buys lesser quantities of goods and services.[76] They buy in small quantities from retailers in the locality who charge higher prices. Sometimes they buy on credit, paying still higher prices. A direct supply of essential consumption goods and services would ensure that basic needs are met first and at a lower cost to society.

This policy further recommends itself on the ground that the consumption of the goods and services supplied under this programme would raise the efficiency and productivity of the labour force thereby increasing social production and raising the income-earning capacity of the poor, thus decreasing the need for income transfers.

This policy too has strong precedents in the *Sunnah* since the *zakāh* on agricultural crops and cattle was collected in kind and distributed in kind. Collections from a region were distributed in the same region, being diverted to other regions only when there were no qualified takers left or when there was greater need somewhere else. The general policy was to supply the poor with a year's supply of food grains.[77] When the Public Treasury began to receive non-*zakāh* revenue, e.g. the spoils of war and *fay'*, the supply programme was also extended to cover the non-poor in the form of annual grants in cash and/or in kind.[78]

It is not necessary, however, that the supply of goods and services under this programme be entirely free of charge to all beneficiaries. Free supplies may be restricted to a target population, while others are obliged to pay for what they receive. Some items may be supplied at a subsidized rate to the poor, others paying the market price. In certain cases, a policy of price restraint may be adopted so that everyone gets the goods or services concerned at a subsidized price. It is not possible, however, to list all the possibilities here. Some options are indicated merely to underline the fact that a specific decision would be needed in each particular case.

It is difficult to draw up a list of items for inclusion in this programme which would suit every Islamic country. Such a list has to be drawn up after examining the needs and resources of the country concerned. But a general recommendation can be made keeping in mind the needs whose fulfilment is required, and the conditions prevailing in underdeveloped Muslim countries. In general, we propose six items for inclusion in such a programme:

- (i) Supply of food grains and other essential consumption goods such as cooking oil, cloth, kerosene oil, sugar, etc.;
- (ii) school meals and milk for children;
- (iii) medical care;
- (iv) education and training;
- (v) transport and communications;
- (vi) housing, including sanitation, electrification and safe drinking water.

The inclusion of these items in a programme for the public

provision of goods and services seems to be necessary for giving effect to the guarantee which is the subject of this study. The problem is how to administer such a programme in countries which lack not only the resources but also the institutional infrastructure for doing so.

(i) *Zakāh,* including *'ushr* or its half (i.e. *zakāh* on agricultural crops) provides a starting point. An Islamic state has to readjust its administrative machinery for the collection and disbursement of *zakāh.* It can form the nucleus for handling the first item in the above list, at least to begin with. The immediate target population should be the rural poor, the surplus being transferred to the urban poor, if any. In the beginning, only such items may be supplied as are actually collected but later on other essential items may also be included, funding their acquisition from the *zakāh* revenue.

(ii) The free supply of milk and lunch packets to small children during school hours goes a long way in fighting malnutrition and ensuring healthy growth. The coverage should be universal but parents with means may be obliged to pay, if necessary. Funding may come partly out of *zakāh* revenue and partly out of general revenue. Milk-cattle collected locally as *zakāh* may be handed over to the local school for supplying free milk to the children. In the absence of a school building the local mosque may serve as the place from where this programme can be implemented.

(iii) Medical care should be provided for all, but its cost may be partly covered by obligatory health insurance contributions from those with incomes above a certain level. This should be the ultimate target, but many of the poor Muslim countries have a long way to go before they can implement such a programme. Details of a phased programme have to be worked out in each country separately. The minimum to begin with is a state-funded hospital in every region supplying free services to the poor. Until such time as this is available, reliance has to be on the income transfers programme which could enable the poor to fulfil their needs from the market.

(iv) Universal literacy and primary education are ends in themselves. But they also make a significant contribution towards reducing poverty – inadequate education is one of the main causes of poverty.[79] Education is also, 'seen as a means of meeting other "core" basic needs (such as adequate nutrition, clean drinking water, and primary health care) . . . mainly because it provides the necessary knowledge for change in current practices and the skills to better use the services provided.'[80] Besides general and Islamic education, there should be special arrangements for vocational training and the creation of skills among the poor. This would help improve earnings, decreasing the burden on income transfers and other anti-poverty programmes. In so far as the beneficiaries are the poor, funding may come out of *zakāh* revenue. It is desirable, however, to offer free primary education to all. At the higher levels, education may be subsidized in varying degrees, depending upon who the beneficiaries are. It is not possible, however, to always restrict the benefits to the poor. Funding has to be out of general tax revenue where benefits flow to the rich and the poor alike, providing cash assistance to students from low income families to see them through higher education.

(v) Free housing may be provided for the very poor from the *zakāh* revenue. Otherwise, a programme of low rent subsidized public housing should be launched for the benefit of low income families. Sanitation may be arranged by local civic authorities financed out of the local rates levied on households with means. A high priority should be attached to the supply of safe drinking water in both urban and rural areas. Wasteful use could be prevented by charging higher rates above a certain level of consumption. The very poor should have access to free supply from public supply points. The avoidance of waste and the proper maintenance of public supplies would require popular participation.

The same principles may apply to electricity and the supply of fuel for cooking and heating wherever needed and feasible. As indicated above, funding may come out of *zakāh* revenue in so far as the beneficiaries qualify for *zakāh,* the remainder being mobilized through additional taxation and the relevant rates charged.

5. *Intervention in the Commodity and Factor Markets*

The state should normally try to ensure fair practices on the part of all economic agents, leaving the prices of commodities and factors to be determined by the market. Intervention may however be necessitated by three considerations: (a) the urgency of need fulfilment, (b) the unbalanced and unjust initial distribution of income and wealth which deprives sections of the population of any access to the market, and (c) the fact that actual markets are never free of corrupt practices. The aim of intervention in the commodity market is to ensure adequate supplies of essential consumption goods and services at reasonable prices. Intervention in the factors market would aim at ensuring fair wages to labour, a fair deal between capital and enterprise, preventing rents from reaching unfair levels and, in the long run, giving effect to the other allocative and redistributive goals of the state's economic policy. The right of the Islamic state to do so in certain cases is fully established in the *Sharī'ah.*[81]

Though the best way to ensure poor people's access to the market is to secure a more equitable distribution of income and wealth, this can only be done in the long run. Meanwhile, 'intervention in the commodity markets to influence both the pattern of output and relative prices is a potentially important instrument of distributive policy.'[82] We have already indicated, in the preceding section, the need to subsidize certain essential consumption goods and services. The diversion of scarce resources from the production of luxuries to that of necessities may call for taxes on the domestic production of certain items or tariffs on their import.

Direct intervention in the labour market is beset with problems. A minimum wage legislation, it is often claimed, may increase unemployment and create more needs than it fulfils. It is difficult, however, to do justice to this issue in this study where we are only considering it in the context of need fulfilment. In any case, an effective programme of income transfers and the public provision of consumption goods would make a minimum wage legislation obsolete.[83] A policy of restraining the prices of wage goods and extending credit and other facilities to small-scale industries is more likely to help the poor by ensuring the greater absorption of labour. 'Small-scale employers tend to use production techniques that are more labour intensive and can more readily employ the less educated labour from the poverty groups.'[84] The rural poor and the urban self employed may be helped by providing them with credit, marketing facilities and such infrastructure as roads, transportation and communication, etc. Public investment programmes may aim to help target populations as well as indicating better techniques. In-job training and skill creation programmes may be given high priority in the public sector and encouraged in the private sector with suitable incentives. Manpower planning and development should go hand in hand with the programmes of income transfers and the public provision of consumption goods to ensure an increase in productivity and earnings.

The prohibition of interest and its replacement by profit sharing is expected to result in a more rational allocation of resources and a more equitable distribution of incremental income. Need fulfilment may, however, require redirecting investment to sectors of the economy catering to basic needs. One way of doing so would be to extend credit facilities to these sectors on more favourable terms. Profit-sharing funds could be supplied to these sectors at lower ratios of profit sharing, i.e. the suppliers of funds claiming a smaller percentage of the actual profits than being claimed in the market. This could be arranged by the Central Bank either by setting up a special agency for this purpose or by providing the commercial banks with suitable incentives for doing so.

Rising urban rents, caused partly by the migration of labour to the urban centres, have often forced the social authority to resort to rent control. But this cannot be a permanent solution, and a more comprehensive approach to the problem is necessary. For the purpose of need fulfilment greater reliance has to be placed on public housing for the poor and the supply of easy credit for house building to the middle income groups.

6. *Ownership and Control of Assets*

A major cause of poverty and need, in which about half the population of Muslim countries finds itself, is the inequitable distribution of land and other income-yielding assets. Redistributive measures are justified on two grounds. Firstly, the existing distribution of land is mostly the result of unjust and un-Islamic practices in the past. Secondly, a reduction in inequality in the distribution of income and wealth is a desired goal of economic policy in Islam.[85] In the context of our study, the guarantee of a minimum level of living to all is best ensured by a more equitable distribution of income-yielding assets in the long run.

'We can distinguish between two approaches in this context: a static redistribution of an existing stock of assets and a dynamic approach aiming at altering patterns of asset accumulation over time.'[86] Land reforms aimed at transforming tenant cultivators into smallholders is one example of the former. Such a policy is recommended by eminent contemporary Islamic thinkers who have also discussed the justification of doing so from the *Sharī'ah* point of view.[87] Another possible measure would be to transfer some shares of the existing joint stock companies and corporations to people with very low incomes. They could be encouraged to do so by making a token contribution out of their own savings, while the rest of the price of these shares could be contributed by the state and the employers. The first target population for such a programme could be employees to whom some shares of the employing corporation may be transferred at concessional rates.

It is easier, however, to channel some of the newly-created income-yielding assets to the poor. This is especially so in the case of public sector enterprises for which capital is acquired by selling shares to the public. Elsewhere we have discussed how shares based on partnership or *muḍārabah* (profit sharing) can be floated for this purpose.[88] We propose that some of these shares be earmarked for the poor. The financing of this project may be from the same sources out of which the income transfers programme is financed.

A sizeable number of the poor earn their living by driving taxis, pulling rickshaws, sewing, etc. In most cases the vehicle or the machine concerned is owned by others, and is hired out to these people. A project to help these people become owners could raise their income-earning capacity. This would require the setting up of some organizations for this purpose and the provision of credit facilities. The agency or organization set up for this purpose could offer, for example, to provide a tailor with a sewing machine on interest-free credit to be paid back in easy instalments. The same principle could be applied to rickshaws, taxis, transport trucks and other mechanical means of self employment. How far *zakāh* funds can be used for financing such a project needs investigation. There is a prima facie case for doing so when the target population is comprised of people entitled to *zakāh* funds.[89]

The pattern of accumulation in the economy which determines the growth of different assets over time can also be influenced in other ways:[90] 'Rural development programmes aimed at providing a balanced addition to (and improvement of) rural infrastructure in the form of land improvement, drainage, small irrigation, feeder roads, credit and marketing institutions and so on, provide one example of this approach.'[91]

Complementary to all efforts, the state should constantly endeavour to improve the educational standards of the poor. In order to increase the income-earning capacity of the poor, more attention should be paid to the creation of useful skills rather than to general education. Similarly, in the context of a basic needs strategy, the problem of descaling (that is, production in smaller units and for scattered markets) will be particularly important, as would the design of new products or adapted products to satisfy basic needs.[92] The training programmes should be designed to produce middle-level technicians and skilled workers needed for implementing such a strategy.

7. *Role of the Private Sector*

A comprehensive need fulfilment programme calls for popular participation at all levels. It especially calls for the active cooperation of the private sector in promoting the appropriate technology, creating job opportunities, providing in-job training, and securing a pattern of output that suits universal need fulfilment. Since profit maximization policies may not always lead to this pattern, and since the price signals cannot guide need fulfilment policies in an economy with an inequitable distribution of purchasing power, there would be a need to rectify the errors of and compensate for the deficiencies at all levels. Since decisions rest on information which can be collected more easily by public agencies, this would entail the private sector being assisted by the Social Authority and the agencies set up by it. Consumers, labourers, and the producers, etc. should also be involved at various levels.

8. *The Need for International Cooperation*

In view of the magnitude of the problem, it would not be possible for most of the poor countries to succeed in guaranteeing universal need fulfilment unaided by the rich countries.[93] Cooperation among all Muslim countries in a region and between the rich and the poor ones on an international level would be required to implement these programmes and to shorten the period of time within which need fulfilment can be ensured on a global level.

Leaving the other dimensions of international cooperation to separate studies, it seems in order to make a general point relating to cooperation among Muslim countries and communities. The texts of the Qur'ān and the *Sunnah* relating to cooperation and to the obligation of the haves towards the have-nots speak of the community as a whole.[94] This obligation cuts across national boundaries, though the first responsibility of any country is its own poor. Suitable measures must, therefore, be adopted for inter-Islamic cooperation in the drive towards universal need fulfilment. Grants, interest-free credit, job opportunities, technical assistance, joint projects for research and development, and trade are some of the numerous possibilities which should be fully explored.

Summary and Conclusion

This brief study has argued that fulfilment of the basic needs of all human beings is one of the primary objectives of organized Islamic living. The principle is rooted in the Islamic worldview and the nature of society and state in Islam. It is established fully in the *Sharī'ah,* being based on texts from the Qur'ān and the *Sunnah,* Caliphal precedents and juristic consensus. Man cannot abrogate or suspend this principle in view of its religious nature. The needs to be fulfilled include food, clothing, shelter, medical care and education. In certain cases they also include transportation, care-taking and attendance. The standard of need fulfilment should depend on the average standard of living in a society and on its economic resources. The individual himself, his near relatives, the neighbourhood and the society in general, each must recognize its responsibilities in this context. But the ultimate responsibility for implementing this principle, in practice, rests with the Islamic state – need fulfilment being *farḍ kifāyah*. The constitution of an Islamic state must contain a clause guaranteeing fulfilment of the basic needs of every human being living within its territorial jurisdiction.

The contemporary situation in Muslim countries calls for a comprehensive approach to the problem. The direct transfer of income to the poor, the public provision of consumer goods and essential services, intervention in the commodity and factors markets with a view to restraining certain prices and ensuring adequate supplies of needed goods, are some of the policy measures which must be taken. The situation also demands a long-term strategy of redistribution so that a more equitable distribution of income and wealth decreases the need for direct transfer. Land reforms aiming at transforming tenant cultivators into small farmers and facilitating the purchase of shares of public sector enterprises by the poor are recommended in this context. Manpower planning and development should accompany need fulfilment in order to raise productivity levels and increase earnings. The private sector has an important role to play in this connection. The resources for funding these programmes may come out of *zakāh* revenue, other state revenue, contributions from beneficiaries with some means, and additional taxes levied for this purpose. Grants and interest-free credit from rich countries to the poor ones are also necessary to implement such a programme. There is a great need for inter-Islamic and international co-operation to help poor countries ensure that their need fulfilment programmes are successful.

Once the necessity of guaranteeing a minimum level of living to every human being is recognized as a part of the Islamic vision, it is hoped that the society as well as its leaders and rulers will be able to mobilize the *will* as well as the *ability* to realize it in practice.

Notes

1. The preservation of one's own life and maintaining it in a state of efficiency is regarded as a duty of the individual (*Farḍ 'ayn*). Says al-Shāṭibī: 'Individually obligatory duties relate to one himself. He is responsible for preserving his religion in belief as well as in practice, and for preserving his life by fulfilling his needs . . .' (Abū Isḥāq al-Shāṭibī: *Al-Muwāfaqāt fī Uṣūl al-Sharī'ah,* Vol. 3 (Egypt, al-Maktabah al-tijārīyah al-Kubrā, n.d.), pp. 176–7.

2. This is clearly implied by the Qur'ānic verse '. . . and be not cast by your own hands to ruin . . .' (2: 95).

3. The Qur'ān 2: 30 and 6: 166.

4. Al-Tirmidhī, *Sunan,* Vol. 4 (Egypt, Musṭafā al-Bābī al-Ḥalabī, 1975), p. 483.

5. See also verses 14: 34, 15: 19, 20, 41: 10, 62: 10 and 67: 15.

6. Al-Nasā'ī, *Sunan,* Kitāb al-Isti'ādhah, Bāb al-Isti'ādhah min sharr al-Kufr, reported by Abū Sa'īd al-Khudrī. The Prophet also prayed: 'Allah, I ask Thy refuge from poverty, scarcity and ignominy.'
Al-Bukhārī: *al-Adab al-Mufrad* (Egypt, al-Maṭba'ah al-Tāziyah, 1349 AH), p. 99, reported by Abū Hurayrah. He prayed: 'Allah, I ask Thy refuge from hunger for it is the worst led fellow.'
Al-Nasā'ī: *Sunan,* Kitāb al-Isti'ādhah, Bāb al-Isti'ādhah min al-Jū', reported by Abū Hurayrah.

7. Al-Nasā'ī, *Sunan,* Kitāb al-Isti'ādhah, Bāb al-Isti'ādhah min al-dhillah, reported by Abū Hurayrah.

8. Al-Khaṭīb al-'Umarī, *Mishkāt al-Maṣābīḥ,* Kitāb al-Buyū'.

9. Abū Dāwūd, *Sunan,* Kitāb al-Ṣalāt, Bāb mā yaqūl al-rajul idhā sallama.

10. Muslim, *Saḥīḥ,* Kitāb al-Birr wa'l-ṣilah wa'-l-ādāb, Bāb al-Nahy 'an al-Taḥāsud wa'l-Tabāghuḍ wa'l-Tadābur.

11. Also see Ibn Hishām, *Sīrat al-Nabī,* Vol. 3 (Bulaq, 1295 AH), p. 76.

12. 'And when it is said unto them: Spend of that wherewith Allah has provided you, those who disbelieve say unto those who believe: Shall we feed those whom Allah, if He willed, would feed? You are in naught else than error manifest' (36: 46).

13. Al-Ḥākim, *al-Mustadrak,* Vol. 2 (Hyderabad, 1340 AH), p. 12 and Aḥmad bin Ḥanbal, *Musnad,* narrations from Ibn 'Umar, tradition number 4880 (edited by A.M. Shākir).

14. Al-Ṭabarānī, *Al-Mu'jam al-Ṣaghīr* (Delhi, Maṭab'at al-Anṣār), p. 91. A similar text has also been reported as a saying of 'Alī himself, see Abū 'Ubayd, *Kitāb al-Amwāl* (Cairo, 1353 AH), p. 595. Hence it is not well established that it is a saying of the Prophet.

15. 'Alī al-Muttaqī, *Kanz al-'Ummāl,* Vol. 3, No. 4761 (Hyderabad, 1312 AH) quoting Ibn al-Najjār, narrated by Anas.

16. Al-Bayhaqī, *al-Sunan al-Kubrā,* Kitāb al-Zakāh, Bāb 'Aṭiyat man Sa'ala bi'l-llāh. Also al-Nasā'ī, *Sunan,* Bāb man Sa'ala bi'l-llāh.

17. The term *fay'* has been used in the early juridical literature to denote all property received from the enemy without actual fighting (as it does in the Qur'ānic verse that follows), land revenue and any revenue other than *Zakāh.*

18. Al-Tirmidhī, *Sunan,* Abwāb al-Farā'iḍ, Bāb mā jā'a fī mīrāth al-māl.

19. Al-Tirmidhī, *Sunan,* Abwāb al-Nikāḥ, Bāb mā Jā'ā lā Nikāḥa illā bil-walī. Also see Abū Dāwūd, *Sunan,* Kitāb al-Nikāḥ, Bāb al-walī.

20. Al-Tirmidhī, *Sunan,* Abwāb al-Farā'id, Bāb mā jā'a man taraka mālan fa li-wārithatihī. Also see Abū 'Ubayd, *Kitāb al-Amwāl* (Cairo, 1353 AH), p. 220.

21. Abū Dāwūd, *Sunan,* Kitāb al-Kharāj wa'l-fay' wa'l-imārah, Bāb fīmā yalzam al-imām.

22. 'Izzuddīn bin 'Abd al-Salām, *Qawā'id al-Aḥkām fī Maṣāliḥ al-Anām,* Vol. 1 (Egypt, Maṭba'ah al-Ḥusaynīyah, 1934), p. 148.

23. *Ibid.*

24. Ibn Kathīr, *al-Bidāyah wa'l-Nihāyah,* Vol. 7 (Cairo, 1939), p. 46.

25. Ibn al-Jawzī, *Sīrat 'Umar bin al-Khaṭṭāb* (Egypt, Maṭba'at al-Sa'ādah, 1924), p. 101.

26. Muḥammad bin Sa'd, *al-Ṭabaqāt al-Kubrā,* Vol. 3, p. 305.

27. Ibn al-Athīr, *Ta'rīkh al-Kāmil,* Vol. 5 (Egypt, Maṭba'at al-Shaikh Aḥmad al-Bābī al-Ḥalabī, 1303 AH), p. 24.

28. Ibn 'Abd al-Ḥakam, *Sīrat 'Umar bin 'Abd al-'Azīz* (Egypt, al-Maṭba'ah al-Raḥmānīyah, 1927), p. 41.

29. Al-Ghazālī, *al-Mustasfā min 'Ilm al-Uṣūl,* Vol. 1 (Egypt, Bulaq, 1322 AH), p. 286.

30. Abū Isḥāq al-Shāṭibī, *op. cit.,* Vol. 1, p. 38. Also see al-Āmidī, *Al-Iḥkām fī Uṣūl al-Aḥkām,* Vol. 3 (Egypt, Maṭba'at al-Ma'ārif), p. 394.

31. Al-Ghazālī, *al-Iqtiṣād fi'l-I'tiqād* (Beirut, Dār al-Amānah, 1969), p. 214.

32. Abū Isḥāq al-Shāṭibī, *op. cit.*, Vol. 2, p. 177.

33. Al-Nawawī, *Minhāj al-Ṭālibīn wa 'Umdat al-Muftīn* (Egypt, Dār iḥyā' al-Kutub al-'Arabiyyah, 1343 AH), p. 125.

34. Ibn Ḥazm, *al-Muḥallā*, Vol. 6 (Egypt, Maṭba'at al-Naḥdah, 1347 AH), p. 156.

35. Al-Ghazālī, *al-Tibr al-Masbūk fī Naṣāi'ḥ al-Mulūk*, (Egypt, al-Maṭba'ah al-Khayrīyah, 1306 AH), p. 94.

36. Al-Jaṣṣāṣ, *Aḥkām al-Qur'ān*, Vol. 3 (al-Maṭba'ah al-Salafiyah, 1395 AH), p. 176.

37. See Muḥammad Bāqir al-Ṣadr, *Iqtiṣādunā* (Beirut, Dār al-Ta'āruf li'l-Maṭbū'āt, 1980), p. 709.

38. Sayyid Abū'l A'lā Mawdūdī, *Ma'āshiyāte-e-Islām* (Lahore, Islamic Publications, 1969), p. 406.
Sayyid Quṭb, *al-'Adālah al-ijtimā'īyah fi'l-Islām* (Beirut, 1967), pp. 240–1.
Muṣṭafā al-Sibā'ī, *Ishtirākiyat al-Islām* (Dimashq, Mu'assasat al-Maṭbū'āt al-'Arabiyah, 1960), p. 203.
Muḥammad Abū Zahrah, *Tanẓīm al-Islām lil-Mujtama'* (Cairo, Dār al-Fikr al-'Arabī, 1975), p. 146.
Muḥammad Bāqir al-Ṣadr, *Iqtiṣādunā, op. cit.*, p. 701.
Muḥammad al-Mubārak, *Niẓām al-Islām, al-Iqtiṣād* (Beirut, Dār al-Fikr, 1980), pp. 133–40.
Yūsuf al-Qaraḍāwi, *Mushkilat al-Faqr wa Kayfa 'Ālajahā al-Islām* (Cairo, Maktabah Wahbah, 1977), p. 121.

39. Yūsuf Ibrāhim Yūsuf, *al-Nafaqāt al-'Āmmah fi'l-Islām* (Cairo, Maṭābi' Diyāb, 1980), p. 229.

40. Al-Bukhārī, *Ṣaḥīḥ*, Kitāb al-Maghāzī, Bāb Ghazwat Dhāt al-Rajī'..., and Muḥammad bin Sa'd, *al-Ṭabaqāt al-Kubrā*, Vol. 2 (Beirut, n.d.), p. 222.

41. Ibn 'Abd al-Barr, *al-Isti'āb fī Ma'rifat al-Ṣaḥābah*, Vol. 1 (Hyderabad, 1318 AH), p. 393.

42. 'Alī al-Muttaqī, *Kanz al-'Ummāl, op. cit.*

43. *Ibid., op. cit.*, Vol. 1, p. 217.

44. Abū 'Ubayd, *op. cit.*, p. 261; Ibn al-Jawzī, Sīrat 'Umar bin 'Abd al-'Azīz, *op. cit.*, p. 74, and Ibn 'Abd al-Ḥakam: *Sīrat 'Umar bin 'Abd al-'Azīz*, p. 167.

45. Muḥammad bin al-Ḥasan al-Shaybānī, *Kitāb al-Āthār*, Bāb Faḍā'il al-Ṣaḥābah (*Ḥadīth* No. 852).

46. Ibn al-Jawzī, *Sīrat 'Umar bin 'Abd al-'Azīz*, pp. 154–5.

47. Ibn Sa'd, *al-Ṭabaqāt al-Kubrā,* Vol. 3, p. 283.

48. Ibn 'Abd al-Ḥakam, *Sīrat 'Umar bin 'Abd al-'Azīz,* p. 67 and Abū 'Ubayd, *Kitāb al-Amwāl,* p. 251.

49. This is a well established principle of Islamic jurisprudence shared by all schools of Islamic law:
Al-Āmidī, *al-Iḥkām fī Uṣūl al-Aḥkām,* Vol. 1 (Egypt, Maṭba'at al-Ma'ārif, 1914) p. 158.
Al-Qurṭubī, *al-Jāmi' li-Aḥkām al-Qur'ān,* Vol. 6 (Cairo, Dār al-Kutub al-Miṣrīyah, 1952), p. 85.
Ibn Taimīyah, *al-Siyāsah al-Shar'īyah* (Egypt, Dār al-Kitāb al-'Arabī, 1955), p. 137.

50. Shihābuddīn Aḥmad al-Ramlī, *Nihāyat al-Muḥtāj ilā Sharḥ al-Minhāj,* Vol. 6 (Egypt, n.d.), p. 194.

51. Al-Bukhārī, *Ṣaḥīḥ,* Kitāb al-Shirkah, Bāb fī Shirkat al-Ṭa'ām.

52. *Ibid.*

53. See Muḥammad al-Ghazālī, *al-Islām wa'l-Manāhij al-Ishtirākīyah* (Cairo, 1951), p. 28.

54. Muḥammad Ibn Sa'd, *al-Ṭabaqāt al-Kubrā,* Vol. 3, p. 317.

55. Al-Qaraḍāwī has quoted Shāfi'ī jurists to the effect that *zakāh* funds may be given to tradesmen for buying the tools of their trade, and to businessmen to replenish their stock (see Yūsuf al-Qaraḍāwī: *Fiqh al-Zakāh* (Beirut, Mu'assasat al-Risālah, 1980), pp. 564–6, 571). In more austere circumstances when no such funds were available, the Prophet adopted a different method to help a needy person learn how to earn his own living:
Anas bin Mālik reports that a man from the *Anṣār* came to the Prophet (peace be upon him) asking (for help). The Prophet asked: 'Don't you have something in your house.' He said: 'Yes, there is a quilt which we partly spread and partly cover ourselves with; and a cup in which we drink water.' He said: 'Bring both to me', so he brought them. The Prophet (peace be upon him) took them in his hand and asked: 'Who buys these?' A man replied, 'I buy both for a dirham.' He said, 'Who can offer more than a dirham?' (This he said) twice or thrice. A man said, 'I buy both for two dirhams.' The Prophet gave them to him and took the two dirhams, which he gave to the man from the *Anṣār* and said: 'Buy food with one of these and give it to your wife and buy a hatchet with the other and bring it to me.' He brought it and the Prophet (peace be upon him) fixed a wooden handle to it with his own hand and said to him: 'Go cut wood and sell it, and let me not see you for the next fifteen days.' The man went on cutting wood and selling it. Then he came and he had earned ten dirhams. He spent some of it on clothes and some of it on food. The Prophet (peace be upon him) said: 'This is better for you than for begging to appear as a blemish on your face on the Day of Judgement. Begging does not suit except three: one in abject poverty, or one under heavy burden of debt or one who has to pay a burdensome blood money.' (Abū Dāwūd: *Sunan,* Kitāb al-Zakāh, Bāb Mā Tajūz fīh al-Mas'alah.)

56. ‘Abd al-Raḥmān al-Jazīrī, *al-Fiqh ‘alā al-madhāhib al-arba‘ah,* Vol. 3, Kitāb al-Ṭalāq, Mabāḥith al-Nafaqāt.
Aḥmad Ibrāhīm Ibrāhīm: *Niẓām al-Nafaqāt fi'l-Sharī‘at al-Islāmīyah* (Cairo, al-Maṭba‘ah al-Salafiyah, 1349 AH).

57. Aḥmad Ibrāhīm Ibrāhīm, *op. cit.*, p. 50.

58. E.g. Yūsuf al-Qaraḍāwī, *Fiqh al-Zakāh* (Beirut, Mu'assasah al-Rīsalah, 1981).

59. Ibn Ḥazm, *al-Muḥallā, op. cit.*

60. Abū Isḥāq al-Shāṭībī, *al-I‘tiṣām,* Vol. 2 (Egypt, Maṭba‘at al-Manār, 1914), pp. 295–8.

61. Al-Ghazālī, *al-Mustasfā,* Vol. 1 (Bulaq, 1322, AH), pp. 303–4.

62. See, Muḥammad bin Aḥmad bin Ayās, *Ta'rīkh Miṣr,* Vol. 1 (Bulaq, 1311 AH), pp. 94–5.

63. Al-Māwardī, *al-Aḥkām al-Sulṭānīyah* (Maṭba‘ah al-Maḥmūdīyah, n.d.), pp. 213–14.

64. Abū Ya‘lā, *al-Aḥkām al-Sulṭānīyah* (Maṭba‘ah al-Bābī al-Ḥalabī, 1356 AH), pp. 273–4.

65. See Ibn Khallikān, *Wafayāt al-A‘yān,* Vol. 6 (Cairo, Maktabah al-Nahḍah, 1948), p. 118.

66. Al-Sarakhsī, *al-Mabsūṭ,* Vol. 10 (Egypt, Maṭba‘at al-Sa‘ādah, 1331, AH), p. 29.

67. Al-Qurṭubī: *al-Jāmi‘ li-Aḥkām al-Qur'ān,* Vol. 2 (Cairo, Dār al-Kutub, al-Miṣrīyah, 1952), p. 242.

68. The right has in fact been regarded by jurists to be justiciable till very recently when steps were taken to bar the courts from admitting such cases. See Abū Zahrah, *Tanẓīm al-Islām li'l-Mujtama‘* (Cairo, Dār al-Fikr al-‘Arabī, 1975), pp. 146–7.

69. See, however, Yūsuf al-Qaraḍawī, *Fiqh al-Zakāh, op. cit.*, pp. 70–1 for other reports about the date of introduction of obligatory *Zakāh.*

70. K.E. Boulding, ‘Allocation and Distribution: The Quarrelsome Twins' in *Value Judgement and Income Distribution,* ed. Robert A. Solo and Charles A. Anderson (Praeger, 1981), p. 162.

71. Paul P. Streeten, *Basic Needs: Some Issues,* World Bank and Shahid Javed Burki: Reprint series 53. Reprinted from *World Development* 6 (1978), p. 418.

72. Richard Perlman, *The Economics of Poverty,* (McGraw Hill Book Co., 1976), p. 215.

73. A Dale Tussing, *Poverty in a Dual Economy* (New York, St. Martin's Press, 1975), p. 140. Also refer to Theodore R. Marmor (ed.) *Poverty Policy – A Compendium of Cash Transfer Proposals* (Chicago, Aldine Atherton Inc., 1971), p. 186. Sheldon Danziger, 'How Income Transfers Affect Work, and the Income Distribution' in Robert Haveman and Robert Potnick, *Journal of Economic Literature,* Vol. xix, No. 3, pp. 975–1028.

74. Paul P. Streeten, 'Basic Needs: Premises and Promises' in *Journal of Policy Modelling,* Vol. 1 (1979), pp. 136–46.

75. ——, 'From Growth to Basic Needs' in *Poverty and Basic Needs* (The World Bank, Sept. 1980), p. 8.

76. Frances Williams (ed.), *Why the Poor Pay More* (London, Macmillan, 1977).

77. Reference may be made to the relevant chapters of *Fiqh al-Zakāh* by Yūsuf al-Qaraḍāwī, (*op. cit.*) on all these points.

78. Abū Yūsuf, *Kitāb al-Kharāj* (Cairo, al-Maṭba'ah al-Salafīyah, 1396, AH), pp. 44–51; Abū 'Ubayd al-Qāsim bin Sallām: *Kitāb al-Amwāl* (Cairo, Dār al-Fikr, 1975), pp. 285–346.

79. Richard Perlman, *op. cit.*

80. Abdun Noor, *Education and Basic Human Needs* (World Bank Staff Working Paper No. 450, 1981), p. 2.

81. For details see Muhammad Nejatullah Siddiqi, *Islām kā Naẓarīyah-e-Milkīyat* (Delhi, Markazī Maktabah Islāmī, 1978), pp. 482–509.

82. Hollis Chenery et al., *Redistribution with Growth* (Oxford University Press, 1975), p. 86.

83. Theodore R. Marmor (ed.), *op. cit.*, p. 181. Also see A. Dale Tussing, *op. cit.*, pp. 215–16.

84. Hollis Chenery et al., *op. cit.*, p. 46.

85. Muhammad Nejatullah Siddiqi, *Islām kā Naẓarīyah-e-Milkīyat, op. cit.*, pp. 441–54.

86. Hollis Chenery et al., *op. cit.*, p. 78.

87. For the opinions of Sayyid Abu'l A'lā Mawdūdī and Ḥasan al-Huḍaibī on this issue, see Muhammad Nejatullah Siddiqi, *Islām kā Naẓarīyah-e-Milkīyat, op. cit.*, pp. 546–52.

88. Muhammad Nejatullah Siddiqi, *Banking Without Interest,* Chapter Seven (Leicester, UK, The Islamic Foundation, 1983).

89. Yūsuf al-Qaraḍāwī, *Fiqh al-Zakāh, op. cit.*, pp. 564–6, 771.

90. Hollis Chenery et al., *op. cit.*, p. 80.

91. *Ibid.*, p. 81.

92. Hans Singer, *Technologies for Basic Needs* (Geneva, ILO, 1977), p. 104.

93. Paul Streeten and Shahid Javed Burki, *op. cit.*, p. 418.

94. The Prophet said: 'The believers in their affection, kindness and loving concern for one another are like the body, (so that) when any one organ of the body suffers the whole body mobilizes itself by developing a temperature and losing sleep.' (Muslim, *Saḥīḥ*, Kitāb al-Birr, Bāb tarāḥum al-Mu'minīn wa ta'āṭufihim wa ta'āḍudihim).

Also see Abū Dāwūd, *Sunan*, Kitāb al-Ādāb, Bāb al-Mu'ākhāt, and al-Bukhārī, *Ṣaḥīḥ*, Kitāb al-Ādāb, Bāb ta'āwun al-Mu'minīn ba'ḍuhum ba'ḍā.

Two verses from the Qur'ān (5: 2) and 9: 71) making the same point have already been quoted in 6 above.

CHAPTER TWO

Public Expenditure in an Islamic State

Introduction

This chapter discusses the principle of public expenditure in an Islamic state. A perspective is set stating the economic goals of the state in Islam: need fulfilment, reduction of inequality and development. Employment, stability and scientific progress are the subsidiary goals to be pursued to ensure fuller realization of the main goals. This discussion is followed by a statement of the functions of the Islamic state which involves three categories under which the main heads of public expenditure are studied:

(i) Permanent heads of expenditure mandated by the *Sharī'ah* which includes defence, law and order, *da'wah,* need fulfilment and the like.
(ii) Expenditure necessary under present circumstances which includes protection of the environment, capital formation and expenditures necessary for stabilization purposes.
(iii) Expenditure required to organize additional activities assigned to the state by its people.

The analysis of public expenditure is followed by a discussion on equitable distribution of the benefits of public expenditure. This is followed by an attempt to construct a theory of public expenditure in Islam based on four overlapping but conceptually distinct planes: explicit command of Allah, *farḍ kifāyah,* market failure and democratic decision by the people. Then we briefly examine the possible adverse effects of public expenditure on the incentive to work and the incentive to save and how this effect can be minimized in the Islamic framework. This is followed by a discussion on the desirability of limiting public expenditure with a view to protecting individual freedom. Then we explore the possibility of assigning priorities to expenditures in the light of the objectives of the *Sharī'ah* and in view of scarcity of resources. In conclusion, we note the wide scope, the clear rationale and the welfare-oriented nature of public expenditure in Islam.

The Perspective

An Islamic state has a purpose. Broadly stated, it is to establish a good society with justice, peace and security, where life flows in accordance with what Allah has willed for man.

> Allah has promised such of you as believe and do good works that He will surely make them to succeed (the present rulers) in the earth even as He caused those who were before them to succeed (others); and that He will surely establish for them their religion which He has approved for them, and will give them in exchange safety after their fear. They serve Me. They ascribe nothing as partner unto Me. Those who disbelieve henceforth, they are the miscreants.[1] Those who, if We give them power in the land, establish worship and pay the poor due and enjoin the right and forbid the wrong. And with Allah rests the final outcome of all events.[2]
>
> We verily sent Our messengers with clear proofs, and revealed to them the Scripture and the Balance, that mankind may observe right measure; and He revealed iron wherein is mighty power and (many) uses for mankind, and that Allah may know him who helps Him and His messengers, though Unseen. Lo! Allah is Strong, Almighty.[3]

The power of the state is to be exercised in a democratic manner, i.e., matters relating to public interest are to be decided in consultation with the people.

> And those who answer the call of their Lord and establish worship, and whose affairs are a matter of counsel, and who spend of what We have bestowed on them.[4]
>
> . . . and consult with them upon the conduct of affairs. And when you are resolved, then put your trust in Allah. Lo! Allah loves those who put their trust in Him.[5]

The rulers should do all that needs to be done for the good of the people. Said the Prophet: 'One to whom Allah entrusts a people [to look after] and he does not serve them sincerely will never get [even] the smell of the paradise.'[6]

'A ruler in charge of the affairs of the Muslims who does not strive for them and serve them sincerely shall not enter the paradise with them.'[7]

On the other hand, it is the duty of individuals to be sincere to the state. The Prophet has said: 'The [essence of] religion is sincerity, the [essence of] religion is sincerity, the [essence of] religion is sincerity.' Asked, 'Sincerity to whom, O messenger of Allah?', he replied, 'To Allah, to His Book, to His Prophet and the society of Muslims and its rulers.'[8]

Within the general framework in which the Islamic state operates it has to aim at three economic goals, besides other social, political and spiritual goals. The three economic goals are need fulfilment, reduction of inequalities, and development. It is neither possible nor necessary to argue this point in detail in this study.

In the previous chapter we have argued in the light of the Qur'ān, the *Sunnah* and precedents from the first four caliphs that an Islamic state is charged with these duties on a permanent basis. It must guarantee fulfilment of basic needs to every human being within its jurisdiction. It must prevent concentration of wealth. It must keep the country strong. Besides these goals, which have a permanent basis in *Sharī'ah,* three more policy objectives assume importance in the context of modern conditions. These are employment, stability and progress in science and technology. Unless these objectives are pursued, it will not be possible to realize the goals of need fulfilment, reduction of inequality and development. Moreover, it is hardly possible, in the present situation, to establish a just economic order without stabilization policies. As regards science and technology, it is not only a precondition for development but also necessary to reduce Muslim countries' dependence on powers hostile to Islam.

It is not the object of this chapter to discuss the goals of an economic system in Islam. We mention these goals in this study of public expenditure in an Islamic state because public expenditure depends on the functions of the state and functions derive from goals. We shall now list the functions of an Islamic state and then study the expenditures that become necessary for discharging these functions. Reference to goals will be made where necessary, and the rationale for each function and expenditure involved will be provided where called for. The basic premise of what follows is that there are certain functions an Islamic state must perform and that the discharge of these functions necessarily involves expenditure. A discussion of the next point, that sufficient revenue has in fact been provided for making these expenditures, is not within the scope of this study.

Rather we will concern ourselves with the expenditure scheme itself: its priorities, distribution of its benefits, its impact on the behaviour of economic agents and on such economic variables as savings and investments, income and employment, etc.

Functions of an Islamic State

The functions of an Islamic state can be classified into three categories:

(i) Functions assigned by *Sharī'ah* on a permanent basis.
(ii) Functions derived from *Sharī'ah* on the basis of *ijtihād* for the present situation.
(iii) Functions assigned to the state at any time and place by the people through the process of *shūrā* (consultation).

The first category includes all functions specified in the Qur'ān and the *Sunnah,* directly or indirectly, and affirmed by the jurists. Society cannot be organized in accordance with Islamic principles unless the state discharges these functions.

These functions relate to the permanent human situation and not to changing social conditions. The objectives of *Sharī'ah* with respect to man cannot be realized without them. Obvious examples are defence and law and order.

The second category includes such functions as have become necessary for realizing the objectives of *Sharī'ah* in view of the social and economic conditions obtaining in our time. They are derived from the Qur'ān and the *Sunnah* on the basis of analogical reasoning (*qiyās*) or by arguments based on public interest (*maṣāliḥ*). But the early jurists have not specified them because the circumstances necessitating them did not exist in their time. An obvious example is protection of the environment, a social problem which has gained eminence in industrial societies with the rise of the modern metropolis. This category is quite flexible, as it depends on time and place. Even at the present time, different Islamic thinkers in different countries may suggest different lists of functions.

This is still more applicable to the third category, which may include any function that the people at any time and place might want an Islamic state to perform. They may even decide to ask the state to do something that the private sector could have done or in fact had been doing. They are also free to reverse such a decision, in the light of experience and on the criterion of what serves the public interest best. Different decisions may be taken in different countries. Take, for example, the generation and supply of electricity. No decisive arguments exist to make it a public-sector industry, to bar the public sector from it or to provide that the public sector and private sector compete in this field. Local considerations relating to resources, costs, etc., may prompt a decision this way or that way. The important thing is that the decision be taken through democratic processes to ensure that it is taken in the public interest.

It is clear from the above that public expenditure in an Islamic state cannot be fixed, neither in quantity nor in terms of heads of expenditure. Public expenditure in an Islamic state is made to perform a function. Since the list of functions is open-ended, public expenditure is also open-ended.

What constrains public expenditure in practice is availability of resources. As public expenditure expands, it becomes necessary to take away private wealth to meet the fundamental values of Islam. A balance has to be struck between securing public interest through public expenditure and ensuring individual freedom. This has been done by subjecting taxation (over and above what is permanently provided in *Sharī'ah*) to the people's consent expressed through *shūrā,* as elaborated in a subsequent section.

We shall now proceed to list the main heads of public expenditure following the three-fold classification noted above.

Permanent Heads of Expenditure

The following heads of expenditure are permanently prescribed by the *Sharī'ah*:

(i) Defence.
(ii) Law and order.
(iii) Justice.
(iv) Need fulfilment.
(v) *Da'wah,* i.e., communicating the message of Allah to mankind.
(vi) Enjoining right conduct and forbidding wrong (*al-amr bi'l-ma'rūf wa'l-nahy 'an al-munkar*).
(vii) Civil administration.
(viii) Fulfilment of such social obligations (*farḍ kifāyah*) as the private sector fails to fulfil.

Maintenance of internal security by enforcing law and order, dispensation of justice and civil administration are the *sine qua non* of organized social living. They are necessary for eliminating corruption (*fasād*) and establishing a just order (*qisṭ*). These duties are addressed to the ruler (*walī al-amr*) who succeeds the Prophet in this task.[9] Individuals are not required, nor even permitted, to implement the penal laws (*ḥudūd*) of Islam to enforce the law.[10] They cannot, on their own, dispense justice among litigants. They cannot assume, without a mandate, the role of civil administrators. These are the prerogatives of the duly established social authority, the *imām* or *walī al-amr*. However, it is a social obligation (*farḍ kifāyah*) that there be a ruler to take charge of these and other duties to be discussed below. Individuals are required to ensure this through a process of mutual consultation. As noted by al-Māwardī:

> Rulership is set up in succession to the Prophet to protect religion and the world. There is a consensus on its being a must to assign it to one who would perform this [duty] . . . Once it is established that having a ruler is a must, [it is to be noted that] it is a duty which is socially obligatory, like *Jihād* and [acquisition of] knowledge.[11]

Defence, need fulfilment, communication of the message of Allah, and enjoining the right and forbidding the wrong are duties explicitly mentioned in the Qur'ān[12] and emphasized in the traditions from the Prophet. Jurists regard them as socially obligatory. Those capable of doing them should come forward and do the needful. But, in view of the crucial importance of these tasks for the physical survival and moral and spiritual progress of the community, the ruler has a special responsibility in this regard. The state has to take the initiative in these tasks irrespective of the role individuals might play. It should not wait to assess the outcome of voluntary efforts so that it can do what remains to be done.

Since there are many other social obligations besides these four, we have included fulfilment of *farḍ kifāyah* in the above list as a catch-all category. To realize the necessity and significance of doing so, a brief discussion on the concept of *farḍ kifāyah* is in order.

Farḍ Kifāyah: Its Nature and Scope

Farḍ Kifāyah is a duty, like the duties of prayer and fasting, with the difference that it is not addressed to an individual but to the community. The Law-Giver wants the duty to be carried out irrespective of who does it. Here is a typical definition:

> They are essential and must be performed, irrespective of who perform them. They include religious duties such as prayers for the deceased [*ṣalāt al-janāzah*] and mundane affairs like the essential industries.[13]

The crucial requirement is that the task must be done: when the objective of the duty is to get the task done, without any regard as to the doer, it is termed *farḍ 'alā al-kifāyah.* Matters covered by socially-obligatory duties generally relate to public interest.[14] This is why even though the responsibility of doing the needful devolves on the community in the first instance, the state has the ultimate responsibility of ensuring that they are done. This has been ably brought out by al-Shāṭibī in the following passage:

> Their being obligatory means that their performance is not the duty of any particular individual but they devolve on the totality of all individuals, so that those common interests are preserved without which individual interests cannot be safe. They reinforce and complete the aforementioned [individually necessary objectives of *Sharī'ah*] hence they are also necessary. Individual objectives cannot be realized without realizing the social ones. Social objectives relate to the good of all men. It is due to this fact that the individual is not specifically charged with these duties and they are not addressed to them, in which case they would have become individual duties. They aim at preserving human life. Individuals are the vicegerents of Allah amidst fellow servants of Allah, to the extent allowed by their abilities and powers. But a single individual has hardly the ability and the power to set his own affairs right, not to mention the affairs of his family, kinsfolk, tribe or the humanity at large. This is why Allah has entrusted the fulfilment of the common needs of mankind to the society as a whole. This is the *raison d'être* of the state in society.[15]

As hinted at by al-Shāṭibī, one of the prime functions of the state is to look after the fulfilment of social obligations on behalf of society. Should individual initiative and voluntary action complete the task, use of authority and the coercive power of the state would not be called for. Failing that, some action will be necessary to get the task done.

It is more harmonious with the ethos of the Islamic system to get social obligations performed by individuals through persuasion. Voluntary associations can be activated, even funded, to organize efforts for doing the needful. However, there may be exceptional circumstances justifying the state taking the initiative. There may be urgency, e.g., in a natural calamity. There may be technical compulsion dictating action, such as supply of weather reports to prevent fatal accidents on roads and due to high seas. Hence, even though fulfilment of a social obligation at public expense and through public functionaries is the last alternative in principle, urgency of the matter or technical compulsion may sometimes make it the only option in practice.

The Qur'ān and the *Sunnah* have not handed down a closed list of social obligations to which no more can be added. They have specified only some of them. The jurists have identified many more by analogical reasoning or on the basis of *maṣlaḥah*. What qualifies an activity for being considered a social obligation is that the vital interests of the people, relating to survival and Islamic living, should depend on it. This is why productive activities on which the fulfilment of basic needs such as food, clothing and shelter depends, have been regarded as *farḍ kifāyah* by the jurists.[16] Since every *farḍ kifāyah* has the potential of involving the state and thereby necessitating some public expenditure, we have included it among the permanent heads of expenditure, as noted above.

Scope of Mandated Expenditures

Some of the heads of expenditure listed above are specifically included among the eight heads of expenditure on which *zakāh* revenue is to be spent, as laid down in the Qur'ān.

> The alms are only for the poor and the needy, and those who collect them, and those whose hearts are to be reconciled, and to free the captives and the debtors and for the cause of Allah and [for] the wayfarers; a duty imposed by Allah. Allah is Knower, Wise.[17]

Hence this verse itself puts items (i), (iv) and (v) of the above list among the permanent heads of expenditure of an Islamic state. To the extent item (vi), *amr bi'l-ma'rūf,* goes with item (v), *da'wah,* it is also included in 'the cause of Allah'. These were also the first to appear in the actual history of Islamic society, soon to be followed by the other heads of expenditure on which revenue from *fay'*[18] and *kharāj*[19] was spent.

The above is noted merely to emphasize that the heads of expenditure listed above are authentic and based on *Sharī'ah*. Otherwise, it is not within the scope of this study to discuss how the revenue necessary to meet these expenditures will be raised. We now proceed to say a few words about some of these heads of expenditure that merit elaboration.

Defence, law and order, judiciary and civil administration are heads of expenditure quite familiar to modern students of public finance. But *da'wah,* or communicating the message of Islam, is unique to an Islamic state. As noted above, communicating the message of Allah to mankind is a collective responsibility of the Muslim people which their state (or states) have to perform on their behalf, side by side with other non-governmental efforts that might be possible. An Islamic state does so first by setting an example and adhering to Islamic principles in the conduct of government and in its relations with the outside world. Second, it can use the media to explain the faith and practice of Islam, reaching the outside world also through the media. It can admit foreign students to universities and educational institutions imparting Islamic education. It can send out scholars and speakers to familiarize people all over the world with Islamic teaching. It can make financial grants to Islamic centres and other institutions abroad engaged in *da'wah* work. An Islamic state should naturally coordinate with other Islamic states in organizing *da'wah* work and activities. We have several precedents, starting from the days of the Prophet himself, of the Islamic state sending out emissaries and scholars to convey the message of Islam outside *Dār al-Islām.*

The sixth head of expenditure, enjoining right conduct and forbidding misconduct (*al-amr bi'l-ma'rūf wa'l-nahy 'an al-munkar*), is a wide category including market regulation, supervision of the common man's behaviour in public places and enforcing Islamic practices in general. Early jurists have dealt with the subject under the title of *al-ḥisbah,* often writing separate treaties on the subject. For a modern Islamic state it will be a matter of convenience whether to put all these functions under one department or divide them into several departments, some of them falling under law and order.

Need fulfilment should cover food, water, clothing, shelter, education and transport.[20] In view of the conditions presently obtaining in most Muslim countries, ensuring even the minimum necessities, would mean a lot of activity on the part of the state. These activities taken together take a large share of public expenditure in a modern state, and this is likely to be the case in an Islamic state also. These activities go far beyond need fulfilment to contribute to economic development and strength of the country. Housing, sewerage, electrification, recreational facilities and other municipal amenities are likely to be included in the same list, though some of them may derive their justification from the functions of state falling under the second or third category noted above, i.e., activities necessitated by present circumstances or those assigned by the people.

It may also be noted that need fulfilment as interpreted by us would cover what some economists have characterized as merit goods, i.e., 'goods the provision of which society [as distinct from the preference of the individual consumer] wishes to encourage'.[21]

The last-mentioned category, *farḍ kifāyah,* requires that there be stand-by arrangements to fill any gaps that might remain, such as building a mosque in a residential area where one is not provided through private initiative. Acting as a watchdog of society, the state will also monitor the economy, with a view to intervening whenever compensatory action becomes necessary to ensure the supply of essential goods and services, etc.

These brief comments should suffice to give an idea of public expenditures mandated by *Sharī'ah*. We now proceed to discuss the heads of expenditures related to the functions of an Islamic state that are derived from *Sharī'ah* with reference to the present situation.

Expenditures Necessary in the Light of *Sharī'ah* in Present Circumstances

These include:

(i) Protection of the environment.
(ii) Supply of necessary public goods other than those included in the first list.
(iii) Scientific research.
(iv) Capital formation and economic development.
(v) Subsidies for priority private activities.
(vi) Expenditure necessitated by stabilization policies.

Scientific research, economic development and stabilization policies have become necessary to build a strong and viable economy in modern times. Muslim countries today lag far behind the advanced countries of the world in scientific research. This is a major cause of the dependence of Muslim countries on advanced countries, some of which are hostile to Islam. Scientific research is also a necessary basis of economic development which is one of the main goals of the Islamic economy. At present the level of national income in most countries is insufficient to provide basic needs for all. Without economic development, it would not be possible to guarantee need fulfilment. Stabilization, i.e., prevention of wide fluctuations in the levels of economic activity, price levels, etc., is necessary to ensure justice and pave the way for economic development. Scientific research and capital formation for economic development call for huge expenditures. Stabilization would sometimes require a decrease in government expenditure to curb inflation, while at other times it might require an increase in government expenditure to boost a sagging economy.

Private economic activities contributing to need fulfilment, *da'wah,* economic development, scientific research and other desired objectives sometimes deserve public encouragement through subsidies. It is a flexible head of expenditure under which provisions may be made according to circumstances, but it is not a necessary head of expenditure like the three others noted above.

Industrialization, urbanization and modern techniques of agriculture tend to disturb the ecological balance and destroy the natural environment created by Allah which is necessary for healthy living. Because of the externalities involved, individuals fail to take this fact into consideration and their actions result in pollution, congestion, etc. Individuals fail to protect the environment, keep the air clean, preserve wildlife, etc., because the costs involved do not match the returns to any particular individual. State action is therefore required to do the needful.

Protection of the environment, scientific research and capital formation (especially the building of infrastructure: roads, bridges, etc.) are public goods, 'which all enjoy in common in the sense that each individual's consumption of such a good leads to no subtraction from any other individual's consumption of the good'.[22] Some of the heads of expenditure included in the permanent list discussed earlier also relate to public goods, e.g., defence, law and order, health, education, etc., since new public goods are continuously emerging and with the progress of civilization it is advisable to include another catch-all head of expenditure in our second list to accommodate them. Consider for example the case of 'information'. Many kinds of information, e.g., weather reports, prices, new developments in medicine, etc., are communicated to the people through radio, television and the press. It is a public good whose inclusion under any of the other heads of expenditure in the two lists given above is not obvious. Flood protection and fire protection are also examples of necessary services whose inclusion under any of the other heads is not obvious. It may therefore be concluded that one of the major heads of expenditure of a modern Islamic state will be the supply of 'public goods' necessary for the well-being of the people. Whether these expenditures can be partly or even wholly financed through fees and charges collected from the beneficiaries and to what extent reliance has to be made on general tax revenue is a discussion that falls beyond our scope.

The above-mentioned heads of expenditure do not find explicit mention in the Qur'ān or the *Sunnah*. Nevertheless, they are necessary according to the unanimous precept of the Islamic jurists that, 'whatever is necessary for discharging a duty is itself a duty'.[23] As we argued above, each of the heads of expenditure in our second list is related to a duty of the Islamic state. These duties are derived from the objectives of *Sharī'ah*: preservation of life, need fulfilment, building a strong community, etc. They can also be supported by arguments based on public interest (*maṣāliḥ*). Some of them also fall in the category of *farḍ kifāyah,* the state being required to do what the private sector fails to do or for technical reasons cannot do. Furthermore, the jurists who have listed the duties of the ruler include many of the items included in the two lists given so far. The two lists given by al-Māwardī cover defence, law and order, *da'wah,* enjoining right conduct, need fulfilment, administration and development.[24] Abū Ya'lā also has a similar list.[25]

Al-Ghazālī has emphasized need fulfilment,[26] and al-Kasānī includes roads and bridges, mosques, rest houses, canals and other public works among the heads of expenditure on which *kharāj* revenue may be spent.[27] Abū Yūsuf includes public works of a developmental nature among the duties of the ruler, even though the modes of financing different works would differ depending upon whether the benefits flow to all or to people of a particular region.[28]

Reciting the duties of the ruler, Imām al-Ḥaramayn al-Juwaynī[29] emphasizes protection of religion, *da'wah,* defence and *jihād,* law and order, dispensation of justice, elimination of corruption and need fulfilment.[30] Discussing the heads of expenditure of public revenue, Ibn Taymīyah includes defence, law and order, justice, civil administration, need fulfilment, grants to the newly converted or even to non-Muslims for promoting the cause of Islam, and salaries to public functionaries including those appointed to call for prayers or lead them. He includes public works like roads, bridges, canals, etc.[31] Shāh Walīullāh al-Dihlawī also includes need fulfilment, defence, law and order, *ḥisbah,* protection and promotion of religion and public works like canals and bridges among the heads of public expenditure.[32]

A survey of the expenditures made from the public treasury during the early period of Islam confirms that all the items on the first list and some of the items on the second list actually figured in government expenditure. The early Islamic state spent revenue on need fulfilment, defence, agricultural development, canals, dams, roads, bridges, buildings, new townships, hospitals, rest houses for travellers, etc.[33]

Expenditure on Activities Assigned by the People

In the two lists given above we have noted some areas that necessarily call for state action. The other activities are left to individuals. Private goods may be produced in the private sector under the overall supervision of the state which will ensure fair practices in the market. Individuals are also free to organize any other activity, individually or in groups, that they think would promote their individual group or societal interests. But individuals are also free to take the position that a particular activity should be assigned to the state. They may do so because the state is better equipped to serve a particular interest, because it will be more cost efficient or for any other reason. Even though it is not desirable to burden the state with too many functions, once a decision is taken through democratic procedure the state should take over the task assigned to it. This is an open-ended category, and different countries may take different decisions according to their circumstances; a decision taken by the people can also be reversed by the people in the light of experience. The decisive factor involved in the people's decision is *maṣlaḥah,* its protection and *mafsadah,* its prevention.

Once a new activity is assigned to the social authority, it is entitled to make the expenditure necessary to organize that activity and raise the required revenue in a manner befitting the nature of the activity, i.e., in the form of taxes where the former is either not feasible or not suitable.

Early Precedents

The possibility that the people may assign the state certain tasks for which they are willing to pay did not entirely escape the attention of the early jurists, even though such eventualities are largely the product of the modern way of living which has created social wants unheard of in the past. The following passage from Abū Yūsuf's *Kitāb al-Kharāj* dating back to the second century after *Hijrah* (eighth century CE) deserves special note:

> I think you should order the people in charge of *kharāj* that when some people from amongst their *kharāj* payers come to them and mention that in their area there are ancient canals that have gone out of use, and lots of uncultivated lands, and that if they clean the canals and excavate them all these lands would become cultivable and productive, ultimately leading to increase in *kharāj* revenue, then they should report it to you. You should depute a person of competence and integrity, who can be trusted in his religion and honesty, to look into the matter. This person should enquire from knowledgeable people of that region who are trustworthy by virtue of their adherence to

religion and honesty. He should also consult experts from outside that region who are not going to benefit from the project or to avert a loss if it is undertaken. If they all agree that it is a good project likely to result in improvement and increase in *kharāj,* you should order digging of those canals all expenses to be met out of the public treasury. Do not charge the expenses from the people of the area concerned because it is better that they develop rather than be ruined. Their prosperity is preferable to their losing wealth and becoming destitutes. Every request from the *kharāj* paying people for repairs, etc., involving improvements and betterment in their lands and canals should be granted as long as it does no harm to others and to the villages and towns adjacent to the area concerned. However, should the project involve harm to others and cause a decrease in their production and decline in their *kharāj,* it should not be granted.

. . . If the people of the Sawād [i.e., Iraq] need digging and cleaning of the big canals which originate from Tigris and Euphrates rivers, you should arrange it for them and defray the expenses partly from the public treasury and partly from the *kharāj* payers. All the expenses should not be charged from the *kharāj* payers. But the canals people dig to their fields, farms, vineyards, orchards, gardens, vegetable plots, etc., should be dug at their own expenses, the public treasury should not bear any part of their cost. As regards the embankments and water outlets on Tigris, Euphrates and similar other large rivers, all expenses relating to their construction and repair shall be from the public treasury. No part of these expenses shall be charged from the *kharāj* payers. Protection of these interests is the duty of the rulers as they are matters relating to the Muslims as a whole. Hence the expenses involved in such works will be from the public treasury because it is by neglecting such works that lands are devastated and ultimately it is the *kharāj* revenue that suffers a decline.[34]

This long passage has been reproduced to emphasize not the obvious point that public works are desirable, but the significant suggestion that the ruler should respond positively to a demand for public works by the people, charging them for the services in so far as the benefits may be specific and localized.

Distribution of the Benefits of Public Expenditure

Public money is a trust. It must not be used for the private benefit of rulers. It must be spent for public purposes. All must be treated equally without any discrimination on any ground whatsoever. This does not preclude, however, taking into consideration need, merit or any other ground of entitlement where it is relevant. Justice should be the hallmark of a public expenditure policy. The Qur'ān says:

> Lo! Allah commands that you restore deposits to their owners, and if you judge between mankind, that you judge justly. Lo! comely is this which Allah admonishes you, Lo! Allah is ever Hearer, Seer.[35]
>
> Oh you who believe! Be steadfast witness for Allah in equity and let not hatred of any people seduce you that you deal not justly. Deal justly, that is nearer to your duty. Observe your duty to Allah. Lo! Allah is informed of what you do.[36]

The Prophet has made it very clear that public money is not to be spent according to the whims of the rulers. He observed: 'I neither give it to you nor deny it from you [on my own]. I am only a trustee, spending where I am ordered to spend.'[37]

'Umar, the second Caliph, has expounded the same principle. 'In my opinion there are only three things to be done with respect to this [public] money. It should be collected with due right, it should be given to whom it is due, and it should be denied improper use. My position *vis-à-vis* your [public] money is similar to that of the guardian of an orphan. If I can afford it I will take nothing out of it, if I need it I will take only what is customarily required.'[38]

Favouritism and discrimination are foreign to Islam. As the Prophet has explained: 'No one has any relation with Allah except through obedience. All men, high as well as lowly, are equal before the law of Allah. Allah is their Lord and they are His servants.'[39]

Apart from inter-personal equity, inter-regional and inter-generational equity are also important considerations in the distribution of the benefits of public expenditure.

Consideration of inter-generational equity is evident in 'Umar's refusal to distribute the lands of Syria and Iraq among those who fought for them. 'Umar rightly cited the Qur'ān's reference to future generations in the list of those entitled to *fay'*-property accruing to the Muslim community by the grace of Allah.[40] As regards inter-regional equity, this, too, was emphasized in 'Umar's policy relating to annual grants. With reference to disbursement of *Zakāh,* it has been laid down that collections from a region should be disbursed in the same region, until its needs are fulfilled. Citing a number of traditions, Abū 'Ubayd concludes:

> All these traditions prove that every people are better entitled to [the revenue of] their *Zakāh* until they don't need it any more . . . The *Sunnah* has provided this because of the importance of neighbourhood and the fact that they [i.e., the local poor] live near the rich.[41]

The concept of equity involved transcends the material to include psychological and moral dimensions. A transfer from the rich to the poor in the same locality or region underlines social cohesion to a degree that can hardly be ensured through global arrangements. Though this provision relates specifically to *Zakāh* revenue, its implications for public expenditure policy in general are obvious; the same principle is to be observed in all public expenditure.[42]

'Umar, the second Caliph, applied the same principle to revenue other than *zakāh*:

> It is my will to the ruler who succeeds me to treat the people in the other regions well. They are the sources of public revenue, the means to thwart the enemy and a shield for all Muslims. He should distribute their *fay'* equitably amongst them and he should not transfer any surplus out of it [to other regions] except by their concurrence.[43]

Unless there is reason for delay, income transfers should be effected speedily, and payments due should be made without delay. The Prophet remarked: 'If I had gold (in the quantity of) mountain of Uḥud I would have liked to distribute all of it before three nights passed, except some quantity reserved for paying any debt that I owed.'[44]

Theory of Public Expenditure

In the light of the above discussion, let us try to develop a theory of public expenditure in Islam. This entails laying down a general framework in which the known particulars fit well and by whose application new particular situations can be adequately handled.

The particulars we have noted can be summarized as follows:

(i) Some public expenditures have been specifically mandated by the *Sharī'ah.*

(ii) Some public expenditures are necessitated by the need to secure public interest. These differ from time to time and place to place and can be derived through *Ijtihād.* Most of them fall into the category of *farḍ kifāyah,* some of them are related to market failure.

(iii) Some public expenditure may arise from tasks assigned to the state by the people.

Some public expenditure may occur in the wake of a stabilization policy in certain circumstances. These belong to category (ii) above.

Any one of these grounds is sufficient to accord legitimacy to public expenditure in an Islamic state. It is possible, however, for some public expenditure to be based on more than one of these grounds. There is also some overlapping of grounds, even though each covers certain expenditures not falling under any of the other heads.

It appears that a package of rationale comprising these grounds (specific mandate from *Sharī'ah, farḍ kifāyah,* provision of public goods, and assignment by the people) can accommodate all known cases of public expenditure in Islam. It also seems capable of accommodating new forms of public expenditure arising from modern conditions. All public expenditure recommended by contemporary Islamic writers on the role of the Islamic state and the Islamic economic system can fit into this framework. It is also capable of explaining all public expenditures undertaken by contemporary Muslim states that have not been disapproved by Islamic scholars.

It can be claimed that any public expenditure that cannot be related to one of the categories listed above cannot enjoy legitimacy, i.e., it has no basis in Islam. It follows that the above provides the touchstone on which public expenditure undertaken by the contemporary Muslim state can be judged with regard to their legitimacy.

We will now have a closer look at the three grounds of public expenditure listed above.

Farḍ Kifāyah and Market Failure

As noted earlier, under normal circumstances a *farḍ kifāyah* becomes the object of public expenditure only when individuals fail to fulfil it. It would, therefore, be illuminating for the purpose of this study to pose the question: Why do individuals fail to do the needful?

A *farḍ kifāyah* may not be performed by individuals due to one or more of the following circumstances:

Lack of Information

Assuming there is a need for individuals to do something that the social interest demands, it is possible that they may simply be unaware that such a need exists. Even if they are aware of the need, it is possible that each individual assumes that others are doing it and therefore the task remains unfulfilled. It is also possible that they realize the need but do not know how one can contribute towards meeting the need, for example, of keeping the air clean or reducing noise levels, etc.

Moral Failure

Individuals may realize a social need exists, they may have the capability to serve that need, but they may not move to do the needful, e.g. a rich man may not feed his hungry neighbour even though he is aware of the situation.

Lack of Resources or Technical Difficulties

Individual resources may not be sufficient to meet the social need involved, or it may be technically impossible to do the needful without collective organization, expert advice or sophisticated equipment, which is beyond the reach of individuals. Defending the country and public health care are obvious examples.

It would be instructive now to look at the causes of market failure as discussed by economists. Very briefly, the foremost cause of market failure is the existence of externalities, i.e. divergence of social marginal costs or benefits and individual marginal costs or benefits. Market failure also occurs in the case of goods whose consumption is non rival, i.e., 'As partaking consumption benefits does not reduce the benefits derived by all others.'[45] Another case of market failure arises 'where consumption is rival but exclusion is not feasible'.[46] This gives rise to the 'free rider' problem – individuals appropriating the benefits but unwilling to pay the costs.

The market mechanism responds to individual preferences based on benefits and costs, and results in private appropriation. It can handle only such goods and services as can be parcelled out among individuals and whose costs can be charged to individuals against the benefits they receive. Hence the goods and services characterized by one or more of the above features, which economists call 'social goods' or 'public goods', cannot be provided by the market. Defence is a good example. The state steps in as an alternative to the market for handling such goods. A political process is substituted for the market to arrange the supply of social goods and allocate the costs involved.

The objects of *farḍ kifāyah* extend far beyond the social goods as defined by economists. Prayers for the deceased (*ṣalāt al-janāzah*) is a *farḍ kifāyah*, but it is not a case of market failure as it is an activity to which the utilitarian cost-benefit calculus does not apply. Fulfilment of the basic needs of the have-nots is also a *farḍ kifāyah* even though the goods and services involved are within the purview of the market mechanism.

Even though all public goods as defined by economists may not be identifiable as objects of *farḍ kifāyah*, and all *farḍ kifāyah* as defined by jurists may not be reducible to provision of some public goods, it is obvious that the two coincide in many cases. This coincidence raises interesting possibilities. *Farḍ kifāyah* is a moral concept. It seeks to replace or in many cases complement the utilitarian benefit cost calculus by an urge to seek the pleasure of Allah by performing a duty. A divergence of social marginal costs or benefits and individual marginal costs or benefits, which causes a breakdown in the market mechanism, does not affect this urge, in so far as it exists. An individual who cares for social interests, over and above his concern for his personal interest, may undertake an activity despite the divergence of social marginal benefits or costs and individual benefits or costs. This creates a possibility of individual action resulting in meeting some social needs that economic theory of public goods sees as being met by the provision of public goods.

It is not necessary, however, that the above individual action works through the market mechanism. It is also not necessary that the market mechanism be replaced by the political process to decide what social goods are produced and how the costs involved are allocated. Individuals may come together in the form of associations and organizations other than the state to undertake some of the activities called for by *farḍ kifāyah*. This is the 'third sector', distinct from the private sector (the market) and the public sector (state undertakings), playing a role in the supply of goods and services. The Islamic institution of *waqf* (charitable endowments) has been doing precisely this throughout Islamic history.

The concept of *farḍ kifāyah* also has some implications for the 'free rider' problem. A sense of duty, as noted above, may make individuals reveal their preferences in bidding for social goods. That is, even though because of non-excludability partaking in consumption is not made contingent on payment, individuals may pay out of a sense of duty.

It is not being asserted that *farḍ kifāyah* would eliminate externalities and do away with market failure. As we have noted above, *farḍ kifāyah* does not cover all public goods. We have also noted a number of reasons why individuals may fail to perform a *farḍ kifāyah*. The above possibilities do, however, exist, and they have important implications. They also explain why activities that are the object of *farḍ kifāyah* are not assigned to the state to begin with, i.e., why individuals are invited to do them in the first instance. As we shall elaborate in a subsequent section, getting the needful done through individual action is preferable as it is more conducive to the protection of freedom.

A theory of public expenditure in Islam should include, therefore, *farḍ kifāyah* as well as provision of public goods as overlapping rationales of public expenditure. Along with this we have a specific mandate from the *Sharī'ah* or from the people, too, as two other bases rationalizing public expenditure. All three grounds are designed to secure public interest (*maṣlaḥah*). An increase in public expenditure as a stabilization measure, may also justify additional expenditure under any of the three heads temporarily. A detailed study of public expenditure for stabilization purposes belongs, however, to a discussion on fiscal policy.

We conclude that all public expenditure in an Islamic economy derives its justification from the relevant activity being explicitly mandated by *Sharī'ah,* by its being a *farḍ kifāyah,* a case of market failure or by its having been assigned to the state by a democratic decision of the people. It is possible for public expenditure to be supported by more than one of these justifications. Any public expenditure which has no basis in any of the above must be regarded as illegitimate and un-Islamic. It is also undemocratic and irrational.

These three bases of public expenditure in an Islamic economy fit well with the three basic postulates on which an Islamic society is founded. These are:

(i) The command of Allah is final, His ownership is absolute.
(ii) All state action should aim at promotion of *maṣlaḥah* (public interest).
(iii) The people's decisions, through a process of *Shūrā,* should govern all matters not already decided in the Qur'ān and the *Sunnah,* explicitly or by implication.

The Incentive to Work

An individual's incentive to work is likely to be weakened by the prospect of his receiving an income without working or of his needs being fulfilled by others. Likewise, taxes levied on incomes in order to finance public expenditure may weaken the incentive to work of those taxed. It is therefore argued that a system of taxes and transfer payment/need fulfilment reduces the total amount of work in the economy, thus reducing production and making the nation poorer.

The danger is real, and the experience of the 'welfare state' in Europe and elsewhere in the West lends credence to the objectives noted above. But critics of the welfare state have failed to come up with an alternative way of dealing with absolute poverty and unfulfilled needs. *Laissez faire* capitalism does not appear to be the answer.

In the framework of an Islamic theory of public expenditure the problem is handled at two levels: motivating the needy individual to work in order to fulfil his own needs and desist from seeking charity as well as motivating the rich individual willingly to give away (as tax and charity) part of his earned income. The concept of *farḍ* (duty) with its two-fold division into *farḍ 'ayn* (individual duty) and *farḍ kifāyah* (collective duty) is designed to create such motivation. Thus, it is an individual duty of those poor who can work to do so and not to seek charity, whereas it is a collective duty of the rich to give away part of their income to provide for the needy.

Several traditions from the Prophet underline these duties as noted below. The Prophet said: 'Charity is not permissible to a rich person or to one who is able bodied'[47] and 'One who asks for charity without being poor is going to eat fire.'[48] Again: 'Asking [for charity] is not permitted except in three cases; a person takes upon himself the payment of indemnity to people, so asking is permitted to him, he asks till he pays up, then he stops; a person is hit by a calamity which wipes out his wealth, so asking is permitted to him, he asks till he gets enough to subsist; and a person is starving and three persons of sound judgement from among his people declare that he is starving, so asking is permitted to him, he asks till he gets enough to subsist.'[49]

The poor who can work were exhorted to work for a living. 'Umar said: 'O poor people! Raise your heads as the road is now clear. Reach out to the good things [of life] and do not become dependent on the Muslims [for your living].'[50]

When people who could work and earn a living did approach the Prophet for charity, he politely refused to oblige. 'Once he was distributing *ṣadaqāt*. Two men approached him to get something out of it. He looked up and found them strongly built. He told them they were not entitled to [receive] it but if they liked he could give them.'[51]

Sometimes the Prophet advised such people how to earn a living. Thus, he made a man sell his quilt and bowl to buy an axe with which to cut wood and earn a living by selling wood. It worked, and the man prospered.[52]

The Prophet made it very clear that earning a living is a religious duty: 'Trying to earn a lawful livelihood is an obligatory duty in addition to the duties which are obligatory.'[53]

Hence the possible disincentive effect regarding work is minimized in two ways. First, those who can work are motivated not to ask for charity but to work and earn their living. Second, the state should not extend support to those who can work and should rather help them find remunerative work.

There seems no alternative to a scheme of income maintenance and need fulfilment through transfer payments and public provision of social goods, taking all possible precautions to minimize the possible adverse effects on the incentive to work.

In an Islamic society the strong stigma attached to reliance on charity seems to be designed partly to mitigate the disincentive effect. How far it goes in a particular Muslim society is, however, a matter of empirical enquiry. There is some evidence that it had a considerable effect on the early Islamic society. Several traditions record that the Prophet's Companions took his advice not to ask for charity very seriously.[54]

Even in contemporary secular societies, empirical evidence on the disincentive effects of these programmes is not conclusive.[55]

The Incentive to Save

There is no reason why a comprehensive public expenditure programme should reduce savings in society. The higher taxes necessitated by these programmes may reduce the savings of the rich in the short run. But a likely effect of such a programme would be to increase the incomes of the poor in the long run which may result in some savings by the poor. This may well compensate for the loss of savings by the rich. Again, empirical evidence relating to contemporary societies with wide-ranging social security and income maintenance programmes is not conclusive.[56] Public expenditure on economic development is likely to raise the national income, resulting in larger savings.

So far as an Islamic society is concerned, there is sufficient emphasis on investments as well as savings in order to provide for one's future needs which prompt even the poor, covered by the social security and income transfer programmes of the state, to save and invest. During the rule of 'Umar, the second Caliph, people received annual grants from the public treasury. One piece of advice that 'Umar gave them was as follows:

> It would be better for these people to buy some sheep out of their grant and leave them [to graze in their fields] in Iraq. When the next annual grant is received they can buy a slave or two and put them to work in these [areas]. This will serve their children as an asset.[57]

To sum up, any tax and transfer scheme has some possible adverse effects on the incentive to work and save. But these effects are not so decisive as to justify abandoning the scheme itself, which is designed to serve some important purposes. Moreover, it is possible to minimize adverse effects by motivating individuals in the manner indicated above. The scheme itself should be so designed as to benefit the poor who are permanently unable to work and earn for themselves. It should also be supplemented by schemes designed to offer work opportunities to those willing to work but unable to find it.

Limits of Public Expenditure

Public expenditure is an important means of realizing the objectives of *Sharī'ah.* In view of the wide scope of these objectives it is not surprising that public expenditure, too, has a wide scope. Nevertheless, one of the important objectives of *Sharī'ah* is the freedom of individuals within the bounds of their obedience to Allah. To be free from fear and tyranny and to obey Allah alone is the ideal of human existence, as indicated in the Qur'ānic verse (24: 55) quoted at the beginning of this paper. Individuals should be able to take their own decisions in economic, political and social affairs as long as these decisions do not infringe on similar rights of other individuals and do not harm the interests of the community in general.

Public expenditure is generally directed towards ends that protect rather than inhibit individual freedom. Defence, law and order, dispensation of justice and civil administration provide security and create conditions in which alone individual freedom can be exercised. *Da'wah* and enjoining right conduct guide action in the right directions and resolve possible conflict between an individual's exercise of freedom. Need fulfilment makes meaningful exercise of freedom possible by relieving the individual from privation. Public expenditure necessitated by social obligations also caters to vital individual and social interests without which individual freedom could not flourish. There is nothing in the permanent heads of public expenditure in Islam, therefore, that poses a threat to freedom.

It is when we come to tasks assigned to the state by the people and to the public provision of social goods and merit goods (other than those covered by permanent heads of expenditure) that some caution has to be exercised. An increase in public expenditure on these grounds would generally involve raising additional revenue through taxation, in so far as the goods or services supplied cannot be priced. Taxation for purposes other than those mandated by *Sharī'ah* or necessitated by social obligation (*farḍ kifāyah*) cannot be levied without the willing consent of the people.[58] Should this consent be available, a possible conflict between individual freedom and public expenditure financed through taxes is resolved, taxation having been endorsed by free choice of the people.

This is not, however, the end of the story. More public expenditure means more public servants and larger bureaucracy – the bane of the modern welfare state. Relative growth in the size of the bureaucracy is not good for the democratic process. Rule by consultation, as required by Islam, is better carried out if fewer people are in the pay of the ruler. It is desirable therefore to minimize the addition to bureaucracy necessitated by the increase in public expenditure due to public provision of social goods and merit goods, and due to other tasks assigned to the state by the people, by getting as many jobs as possible done by the private sector and the 'third sector'. Public provision of goods or services does not necessarily require its production in the public sector. Education, medical services, housing, etc., may be made available to the deserving at cheaper rates, or even free, without producing these services in the public sector. A system of subsidies and transfers can be used to achieve the desired ends.

Ultimately, political decision-making through consultation will decide the actual limits to what the state must do. A formulation of Islamic economic policy can only note guiding principles. Some of these are provided in the form of the priorities discernible from *Sharī'ah.*

Before we discuss the priorities, it should be noted that the Islamic injunctions against extravagance (*iḍā'at al-māl*) and expenditure on prohibited activities (*tabdhīr*) studied in detail elsewhere[59] apply to both public expenditure and private expenditure. The state must economize. Public money should be managed as a trust fund. All property is a trust, but public property is doubly so. Those who manage it are accountable to Allah as well as to the people.

Priorities in Public Expenditure

Jurists have distinguished between the necessary (*ḍarūrī*), the needed (*ḥājī*), and the commendable (*taḥsīnī*) among the interests (*maṣāliḥ*) that *Sharī'ah* seeks to protect. The necessary takes precedence over the needed, which complements it, whereas the commendable complements the needed category of interests. Al-Shāṭibī states that the necessary interests that are protected are related to the following five:

dīn (religion);
nafs (life or self);
'aql (intellect or reason);
nasl (family or progeny) and
māl (property).[60]

Al-Ghazālī also regards the protection of these five interests to be the objectives of *Sharī'ah*[61] and so does al-Āmidī.[62] In so far as the public expenditures required for these purposes have been specified by *Sharī'ah* as is the case with the permanent heads of expenditure listed earlier, the priorities are clear. Beyond that the matter is left to *ijtihād,* and recourse to the political process of decision by consultation becomes necessary.

Al-Shāṭibī rightly observes that in order to fully protect vital human interests, one should not stop at the necessary; it is advisable to ensure the needed (*ḥājī*) to reinforce the necessary (*ḍarūrī*).[63] To what extent the social authority is able to do so would obviously depend on the availability of resources. To the extent it involves additional taxation, the consent of those taxed is necessary, and we are once again led to the political process. Even in the context of necessary interests, the quantitative aspects of public expenditures can be decided only with reference to a particular time and place. It is therefore a matter to be left to *ijtihād*. Decisions involving public interest that are left to *ijtihād* cannot be taken by individuals. They require the consultative process. Hence the only way to decide the volume of public expenditures is democratic decision-making at the appropriate level.

We conclude, therefore, that *Sharī'ah* does provide broad guidelines in the light of which it will be possible for a modern Islamic state to decide on priorities in public expenditure through a democratic process.

Conclusion

Public expenditure in an Islamic state has a wide scope. It derives its legitimacy from the explicit and implicit provisions of *Sharī'ah* and the democratic decisions of the people. Its actual scope is determined by *maṣlaḥah* (public interest), market failure and the will of the people. It is intended to serve all, equitably and without discrimination. It is directed towards eliminating poverty, reducing inequality and building a strong and developed economy. It is expected to promote the welfare of the people without impairing their will to work, save and invest. There is, however, a need to limit public expenditure with a view to minimizing state control and protecting individual freedom. Public expenditure should be subjected to the priorities of *Sharī'ah* and decided in consultation with the people, especially when it involves additional taxation.

Notes

1. *Al-Nūr* 24: 55; translations of all verses from the Qur'ān are taken from M.M. Pickthall, *The Meaning of the Glorious Qur'ān* (Makkah, The Muslim World League, 1977), unless otherwise specified.

2. *Al-Ḥajj* 22: 41; Pickthall's translation partly modified; see Abdullah Yusuf Ali, *The Glorious Qur'ān, Translation and Commentary* (Leicester, The Islamic Foundation, 1978) and Muhammad Asad, *The Message of the Qur'ān* (London, E.J. Brill, 1980).

3. *Al-Ḥadīd* 57: 25.

4. *Al-Shūrā* 42: 38.

5. *Āl 'Imrān* 3: 159.

6. Al-Bukhārī, Muḥammad bin Ismā'īl, *al-Saḥīḥ,* Kitāb al-Aḥkām, Bāb Man Istar'ā Ra'ayatan Thumma Lam Yanṣaḥ.

7. Abū 'Awānah, *Musnad,* Vol. 1 (Hyderabad, Dā'irat al-Ma'ārif, 1362 AH), p. 32.

8. Abū Dāwūd, *Sunan,* Kitāb al-Ādāb, Bāb al-Naṣīḥah.

9. Ibn Khaldūn, *al-Muqaddimah* (Beirut, Dār al-Kutub al-Lubnānī, 1982), pp. 338–9.

10. '*Sharī'ah* has a number of laws that cannot be implemented except by the ruler or one who governs on behalf of the ruler, such as implementing *ḥudūd* on free persons' (Ibn Ṭāhir al-Baghdādī, 'Abd al-Qāhir, *Kitāb Uṣūl al-Dīn* (Beirut, Dār al-Kutub al-'Ilmīyah, 1981), p. 272).

11. Al-Māwardī, 'Alī bin Muḥammad, *al-Aḥkām al-Sulṭānīyah* (Beirut, Dār al-Fikr, 1974).

12. To note only a few verses, we find mention of defence in *al-Anfāl* 8: 60, *al-Baqarah* 2: 190–3 and *al-Nisā'* 4: 75–5; need fulfilment in *al-Dhāriyāt* 51: 19, *al-Ma'ārij* 70: 24–5 and *al-Ḥadīd* 57: 7; *da'wah* and *amr bi'l-ma'rūf* in *al-Baqarah* 2: 143, *al-Ḥajj* 22: 41, *Āl 'Imrān* 3: 110 and *al-Tawbah* 9: 71.

13. Ibn Amīr al-Ḥājj, *al-Taqrīr wa'l-Taḥbīr (Sharḥ Kitāb al-Taḥrīr),* Vol. 2 (Bulaq, 1316 AH), p. 135.

14. Al-Zarkashī, *al-Manthūr fi'l-Qawā'id,* Vol. 3 (Kuwait, Ministry of Awkaf, 1982), p. 33.

15. Al-Shāṭibī, Abū Isḥāq, *al-Muwāfaqāt fī Uṣūl al-Sharī'ah,* Vol. 2 (Cairo, al-Maktabah al-Tijāriyah, n.d.), p. 177.

16. Ibn Taymīyah, *Majmū' Fatāwā Shaykh al-Islām Aḥmad bin Taymīyah,* Vol. 29 (Riyāḍ, Al-Riyāḍ Press, 1383 AH), p. 194; Ibn Taymīyah, *al-Ḥisbah fi'l-Islām* (Kuwait, Maktabat, Dār al-Arqam, 1983), pp. 26–9; al-Nawawī, *Minhāj al-Ṭālibīn wa 'Umdat al-Muftīn,* Vol. 6 (Cairo, Dār Iḥyā' al-Kutub al-'Arabī, 1318 AH), p. 194; Ibn 'Ābidīn, *Ḥāshiyat Radd al-Muḥtār,* Vol. 1 (Cairo, al-Maṭba'ah al-Maymanīyah, 1318 AH), p. 32; al-Zarkashī, Vol. 3, p. 37.

17. *Al-Tawbah* 9: 60.

18. *Fay'* includes all property received from the enemy without actual fighting, land revenue and many revenues other than *zakāh,* e.g. property left without an heir or lost and found to be without an owner. Thus *kharāj*, which means land tax, is included in the broad meaning of *fay'*.

19. *Ibid.*

20. For detailed *Sharī'ah* arguments in support of this list see the previous chapter.

21. Richard A. Musgrave and Peggy B. Musgrave, *Public Finance in Theory and Practice* (McGraw Hill, 1984), p. 78.

22. Paul A. Samuelson, *The Collective Scientific Papers of Paul A. Samuelson,* ed. Joseph E. Stiglitz (Oxford & IBH Publishing Co., 1966), p. 1223.

23. Ibn Taymīyah, *al-Siyāsah al-Shar'īyah fī Aḥwāl al-Rā'ī wa'l-Ra'īyah* (Beirut, Dār al-Ma'rifah, 1969), p. 137; al-Qurṭubī, Abū 'Abdullāh, *al-Jāmi'li-Aḥkām al-Qur'ān,* Vol. 6 (Cairo, Dār al-Kutub al-Miṣrīyah, 1952), p. 85; al-Āmidī, Sayfuddīn, *al-Aḥkām fī uṣūl al-Aḥkām,* Vol. 1 (Beirut, Dār al-Kutub al-'Ilmīyah, 1980), p. 158; al-Sarakhsī, Shamsuddīn, *Kitāb al-Mabsūṭ,* Vol. 30 (Beirut, Dār al-Ma'rifah, 3rd. Print, n.d.), p. 251.

24. Al-Māwardī, *Kitāb Ādāb al-Dunyā Wa'l-Dīn* (Beirut, Dār Iḥyā' al-Turāth al-'Arabī, 1979), pp. 116–17.

25. Abū Ya'lā, *al-Aḥkām al-Sulṭānīyah* (Dār al-Fikr, 1974), pp. 27–8.

26. Al-Ghazālī, Abū Ḥāmid, *al-Tibr al-Masbūk fī Nasīḥat al-Mulūk* (Egypt, Maktabah al-Jundī, 1967), p. 105.

27. Al-Kāsānī, Abū Bakr bin Mas'ūd, *Badā'i' wa'l-al-Ṣanā'i' fī Tartīb al-Sharā'i',* Vol. 2 (Egypt, al-Matba'ah al-Jamālīyah, 1910), p. 62.

28. Abū Yūsuf, *Kitāb al-Kharāj* (Cairo, al-Maṭba'ah al-Salafīyah, 1397 AH), pp. 118–19.

29. Imām al-Ḥaramayn al-Juwaynī, 'Abd al-Malik bin 'Abd Allāh, *Ghiyāth al-Umam fī Iltiyāth al-Ẓulam* (Cairo, Maṭba'ah Nandāh Miṣr, 1401 AH), pp. 184–236.

30. *Ibid.*, pp. 250–70.

31. Ibn Taymīyah, *al-Siyāsah al-Shar'īyah* . . . (Beirut, Dār al-Ma'rifah, 1967), pp. 50–62.

32. Al-Dihlawī, Shāh Walīullāh, *Ḥujjatullāh al-Bālighah,* Vol. 2 (Beirut, Dār al-Ma'rifah, n.d.), p. 177.

33. Hasan-Uz-Zaman, S.M., *The Economic Functions of the Early Islamic State* (Karachi, International Islamic Publishers, 1981), pp. 186–321.

34. Abū Yūsuf, *op. cit.,* pp. 118–19.

35. *Al-Nisā'* 4: 58

36. *Al-Mā'idah* 5: 8

37. Abū Dāwūd, Kitāb al-Kharāj wa'l-fay' wa'l-Imārah, Bāb fī mā Yalzam al-Imām min Amr al-Ra'īyah.

38. Abū Yūsuf, *op. cit.,* p. 127.

39. Ibn Kathīr, Ismā'īl bin 'Umar, *al-Bidāyah wa'l-Nihāyah,* Vol. 7 (Cairo, Maṭba'at Sa'ādah, 1935), p. 35.

40. *Al-Ḥashr* 59: 10

41. Abū 'Ubayd al-Qāsim bin Sallām, *Kitāb al-Amwāl* (Beirut, Dār al-Fikr, 1975), p. 711.

42. Yūsuf, Ibrāhīm Yūsuf, *al-Nafaqāt al-'Āmmah fī'l-Islām; Dirāsah Muqāranah* (Cairo, Dār al-Kutub al-Jāmi'ī, 1980), pp. 170–4.

43. Yaḥyā bin Ādam, *Kitāb al-Kharāj* (Cairo, al-Matba'ah al-Salafiyah, 1347 AH), p. 67.

44. Abū 'Ubayd al-Qāsim bin Sallām, *op. cit.,* p. 316.

45. Musgrave, *op. cit.,* p. 49.

46. *Ibid.*

47. Abū 'Ubayd, *op. cit.,* p. 69.

48. *Ibid.,* p. 663.

49. Abū Dāwūd, Kitāb al-Zakāt, Bāb Mā Tajūzu Fīh al-Mas'alah.

50. Al-Kattānī, 'Abd al-Ḥayy bin 'Abd al-Kabīr, *Niẓām al-Hukūmah al-Nabawīyah al-Musammā al-Tarātīb al-Idārīyah,* Vol. 2 (Beirut, Dār al-Kutub al-'Arabī, n.d.), p. 23.

51. Al-Sarakhsī, *op. cit.,* Vol. 30, p. 271.

52. Abū Dāwūd, Kitāb al-Zakāt, Bāb Mā Tajūzu Fīh al-Mas'alah.

53. Al-Khaṭīb, al-'Umarī, *Mishkāt al-Maṣābīḥ,* Kitāb al-Buyū' Bāb al-Kasb wa'l-Ṭalab al-Ḥalāl.

54. Abū Dāwūd, *op. cit.,* Kitāb al-Zakāt, Bāb Karāhiyat al-Mas'alah.

55. A. Dale Tussing, *Poverty in a Dual Economy* (New York, St. Martin's Press, 1975), p. 140; Richard Perlman, *The Economics of Poverty* (McGraw Hill Book Co., 1976), pp. 210, 215; Richard B. Mackenzie and Gordon Tullock, *The World of Economics: Explorations into Human Experience* (London, Richard D. Irwin Inc., 1975), p. 186; Arthur M. Okun, *Equality and Efficiency: The Big Trade Off* (Washington DC, The Brookings Institution, 1975), pp. 69–97; Edmund S. Phelps (ed.), *Private Wants and Public Needs* (New York, W.W. Norton & Company, 1965), pp. 55–65.

56. Okun, *op. cit.,* pp. 55–65.

57. Al-Balādhurī, Aḥmad bin Yaḥyā bin Jābir, *Futūḥ al-Buldān* (Cairo, Maṭba'ah al-Mausū'ah, 1932), p. 439.

58. It is in this context that the rule laid down by the Prophet, 'A man's property cannot be taken away except through his willing consent', becomes pertinent. See Aḥmad bin Ḥanbal, *Musnad,* Vol. 5 (Beirut, al-Maktabah al-Islāmī, n.d.), p. 73.

59. See Chapter 5.

60. Al-Shāṭibī, *op. cit.,* p. 19.

61. Al-Ghazālī, *al-Mustasfā min 'Ilm al-Uṣūl,* Vol. 1 (Bulaq, al-Maṭba'ah al-Amīrīyah, 1322 AH), p. 287.

62. Al-Āmidī, *op. cit.,* Vol. 3, p. 394.

63. Al-Shāṭibī, *op. cit.,* p. 17.

CHAPTER THREE

Public Borrowing in Early Islamic History

Introduction

Public borrowing has assumed great importance in recent years as indicated by the phenomenal rise in the volume of domestic as well as external debt. This is especially true of the Muslim countries most of which belong to the group of poor developing countries of the world. There is a growing literature on the 'solution' to the crisis supposedly faced by the world financial system because of these debts; some of which is now considered to be unrepayable. There have been attempts to look at the causes of this phenomenon of permanent indebtedness of nations. Islamic economists have also discussed the implications of abolition of interest for public borrowing. They have tried to find alternative ways of financing public needs hitherto financed by borrowing.

It is in this context that scholars have felt the need to look back and see what lessons can be learnt from the Islamic heritage. Did the Islamic state in the past borrow? If so, why and how, i.e. on what terms? Were there any alternatives to borrowing? With these and related questions one can explore the historical records of the many governments, spanning vast regions of the globe over the long period of fourteen hundred years. This is however, a very ambitious project requiring extensive teamwork. Yet another problem with such a study is the authenticity of what the Muslim rulers have been doing all these centuries in these regions. Authenticity naturally belongs to the decisions and actions of the Prophet. The consensus of the community has extended this authenticity to the period of the four pious Caliphs also, i.e. to the policies of the Islamic state till the year 40 after *Hijrah*.

In other words, in the context of public finance (including public borrowing) the policies of the Islamic state till the fortieth year after *Hijrah* can serve as examples of Islamic policy-making and, taking into consideration other relevant factors such as need, scope and perceived functions of borrowing, etc. and as a guide to Islamic statecraft in the modern period. As regards the other Muslim rulers, their decisions and policies have to be judged on the criteria of the Qur'ān and the *Sunnah*. In the context of public borrowing, the most important criterion on which the legitimacy of public borrowing by Muslim rulers has to be judged is prohibition of interest. This means that if an incidence of borrowing on the basis of interest by a Muslim ruler is reported, it has to be regarded as an aberration rather than a precedent, generally speaking. This does not mean, however, that recording and analyzing such cases is of no use to Islamic economists. There is a possibility that such a course of action was resorted to under 'extreme necessity' (*iḍṭirār*). In this case it becomes possible to condone the action despite the fact that it cannot be a precedent for others, being a violation of *Sharī'ah*. While a judgement in such cases may be beyond the scope of an Islamic economist's vocation, it is his job to study these cases and analyze the causes and consequences as befits an economic historian. In fact such a study on his part will not only facilitate proper 'judgement' on such matters, it is a necessary precondition to it.

Another important dimension of the matter is the linkage of a particular policy decision with the realization of the goals of *Sharī'ah*. Did public borrowing serve a well recognized goal of *Sharī'ah*, is an obvious criterion on which its propriety or otherwise should be judged.

This study covers only the periods of the Prophet, the four pious Caliphs, the Umayyads and that of the 'Abbāsids till 333 AH/944 CE after which real power passed, in succession, to the Buwaihids and the Seljuks, and this continued till the sacking of Baghdad by Holaku in 656/1258 which put an end to the 'Abbāsid Caliphate at Baghdad.

Our primary task has been to record the reported cases of borrowing by the ruler for public purposes. Then we look into such details as the need and circumstances which prompted borrowing, the amount borrowed (in cash or kind), the identity of the lender, the terms and conditions attached, if any. We also inquire whether the lending was voluntary or the ruler had to coerce the lender. If available we also look at the details of the repayment of the loan. Having noted these features we try to analyze these cases in relation to their causes and consequences. Finally, we ponder over the lessons that can be drawn, if any.

A serious handicap faced by the writer has been the absence of any other study on the subject which could help in posing the questions or searching for the answers. This should be regarded as one of the reasons should the discerning reader find the present study deficient in any way.

Public Borrowing by the Prophet

The Prophet is known to have been a frequent borrower in his private capacity at least in the difficult early years in Madīnah, but reports relating to these borrowings do not concern us in this study. We have noted only those cases where the Prophet borrowed as the leader of the Muslims and head of the state he established at Madīnah. It is not at all difficult to distinguish between the Prophet's personal borrowing and his borrowing for public purposes since the texts themselves facilitate such a distinction.

Our search has so far led us to six cases of public borrowing by the Prophet, which are reported below. A possible seventh case will also be noted.

(1) We first present a report by Bilāl, a life-long Companion of the Prophet who spent most of his time near the Prophet from the early Makkan period till the Prophet breathed his last in Madīnah. This report tells us that the Prophet used to borrow frequently in order to help needy Muslims whenever the circumstances called for doing so. Though this borrowing would be for comparatively small amounts, in cash or kind, the borrowing was done even when no means of repayment were in sight.

It is reported of Zayd that he heard Abū Salmān saying that 'Abdullāh al-Hawāzānī told him: 'I met Bilāl, who used to give call for prayers for the Messenger of Allah, at Ḥalab. I asked him to narrate about the expenditures of the Messenger of Allah. He said: "He did not have anything (to spend).[1] I used to look after it on his behalf ever since Allah called him to prophethood till his death. It was his practice that when a man came to him as a Muslim and he saw him in need of clothes he would order me and I would go and borrow and buy a cloak for him, clothe him and feed him. This continued till a person from amongst the polytheists accosted me and said: 'O Bilāl, I have enough resources so you do not borrow from anyone other than me.' I did accordingly. One day it so happened that, as I made ablution and rose to give the call for prayer, that polytheist came along accompanied by a group of traders. When he saw me he called, 'O Abyssinian!' I said, 'yes'. He presented a grim face to me and addressed me harshly, saying: 'Do you know how many days are left between you and the (end of the) month (when repayment is due)?' Bilāl said, 'I told him it is near.' He said, 'It is only four days between you and it, after which I will capture you against what you owe and return you to grazing sheep as you used to do before.' I felt what people feel (on hearing such a threat). When I had prayed the night prayer (i.e. *'Ishā'*) and the Prophet retired to his family, I sought permission to see him. He admitted me in. I said: 'O Messenger of Allah, you are dearer to me than my father and mother, the polytheist from whom I used to borrow has said this and that, and you do not have the means to repay him, nor do have I. He is going to humiliate me. Please permit me to abscond to one of these tribes (outside Madīnah) who have accepted Islam till such time as Allah provides to His Messenger, from out of which provision he can pay back the loan.' I came out (of the Prophet's place) till I reached my home and put in readiness my sword, socks, shoes and shield at the head of my bed. When the first light of dawn appeared on the horizon I got ready to go. Suddenly I heard a man calling. 'O Bilāl! you are to report (immediately) to the Messenger of Allah, peace be

> unto him.' I set off till I came to him. What I saw there were four camels resting with their loads. I sought permission to see (the Prophet). The Messenger of Allah, told me, 'Cheer up, Allah has sent what you can pay back your loan with!' Then be asked, 'Did you not notice the four camels in rest?' I said that I did. He said, 'You have the camels as well as their loads. They are laden with clothes and food which have been presented to me by the chieftain of Fidak. Take possession of them and pay off your debt.' I did accordingly . . . .'' '[2]

This incident should belong to the sixth year after the *Hijrah,* or the period after that, since Fidak was subdued during that period.

The one important point emerging from this report is the primacy attached to need fulfilment. It was regarded by the Prophet to be a purpose important enough to borrow even from non-Muslims and without any definite means of repayment in sight.

(2) The second report is not explicit as to the purpose of borrowing but there are clear indications of the loan being repaid out of the public treasury. This presumes borrowing for some public purpose. As the details in the Arabic text reveal, the report reproduced below is part of the story of a Jewish person in Madīnah who embraced Islam. This person to whom the Prophet owed (a quantity of dates, most probably) wanted to test the Prophet's self control and forbearance. Hence his peculiar behaviour.

> . . . Zayd bin Si'nah said: 'When the due date of the loan was only two or three days away, the Prophet came to attend the funeral procession of a man from the *Anṣār,* accompanied by Abū Bakr, 'Umar, 'Uthmān and some other Companions. When, after saying the funeral prayers, he came near a wall to sit by it, I came to him and gave him a very hard look. I took hold of his shirt and the outer robe and said: ''Pay up to me, O Muḥammad! By God, what I know about default on the part of you children of 'Abd al-Muṭṭalib is based on my direct contacts with you people!'' Then I looked towards 'Umar whose eyes were moving in

his face like the rotation of the heavenly bodies. He looked towards me and said: ''O Jew!, you do this to the Messenger of Allah? By him Who sent him down with truth I would have struck your head with my sword but for that I fear to miss.'' (Zayd) said: 'The Messenger of Allah, was calmly looking at 'Umar and smiling. Then he said: ''Myself and he are in need of something else (from you), that you advise me to pay back gracefully and advise him to ask for repayment politely. O 'Umar, go and pay back what is due to him and give an additional twenty *sa'* of dates against your threat to him.'' '

Then (Zayd, son of Si'nah) narrated how he embraced Islam.[3]

(3) We now report a case in which borrowing by the Prophet may have been for private purposes. However, there is some likelihood of the debt having been incurred to meet some public need.

Abū Sa'īd al-Khudhrī reports that a bedouin came to the Prophet, asking for repayment of a debt owed by him. He behaved rudely and said: 'I will continue insisting till you have paid up.' Thereupon the Companions scolded him and said: 'Woe upon you, do you know whom you are addressing?' He said: 'I am only claiming my rights.' The Prophet said: 'Why did not you side with him who had the rightful claim?' Then he sent a message to Khawlah, daughter of Qays, that if she had some dates she should lend it to him till his own dates arrived out of which he could pay back to her. She responded by saying: 'Yes, you are dearer to me than my father, O Messenger of Allah!' (The narrator says) so she lent to him and he paid up to the bedouin and presented some food to him. Thereupon he said: 'You have fulfilled your obligation, may Allah repay you well.' The Prophet then said: 'These are the best of the people. A community in which the weak cannot get his due right without trouble will not be regarded as pure.'[4]

The phrase 'till our dates arrive' most probably refers to the annual share from Khaybar out of which a fifth was earmarked for the family of the Prophet and the rest for other beneficiaries. These shares would naturally be channelled through the public treasury. That the dates lent by Khawlah were to be repaid out of the dates coming from Khaybar leaves both possibilities open: It could be paid out of the fifth assigned to the Prophet's family, in which case the loan would have been a private loan. Equally possible, it could have been paid out of the part earmarked for other beneficiaries, in which case the original debt must have been incurred in order to meet the urgent needs of the same beneficiaries.

A significant point to be noted in the above report is the practice of obtaining a loan in order to pay back an earlier one.

As distinguished from the first two cases, in this case the lender was a Muslim. The second lender, whose lending made possible the repayment to the first lender, was also a Muslim.

(4) The fourth case is a case of borrowing in kind, the object being a camel of a particular age. Repayment was made from out of the camels collected as *zakāh*. This rules out the possibility of the loan being in the Prophet's personal capacity since he was barred from *zakāh*.

> 'Abū Rāfi' reports that the Prophet borrowed a small camel from a man. Then some camels from out of those collected as *Zakāh* came to him and he asked Abū Rāfi' to pay back to the man the camel (owed to him). Abū Rāfi' came back and said he could find only better camels (older in age) who had their four teeth grown. He (the Prophet) said: 'Give it to him. The best among people are those who are good at paying back.'[5]

As noted by Ibn Ḥajar al-'Asqalānī[6] while commenting upon a version of the same *ḥadīth* in al-Bukhārī's *Ṣaḥīḥ*, this debt was most probably incurred for helping somebody meet his basic needs.

The main point that emerges from this case is the propriety of borrowing for public purposes when there is a definite source of revenue in sight. The Prophet borrowed for need fulfilment intending to repay from *zakāh* to be realized in the future.

(5) In the fifth case to be reported the purpose of borrowing was to meet the requirements of *jihād* – war in the cause of Allah. This occurred on the eve of the battle of Ḥunayn in the eighth year after *Hijrah*.

> When the Messenger of Allah, decided to march up on Hawāzin to meet them (in battle) he was informed that Ṣafwān bin Umayyah had coats of arms and other weapons. He sent for him – still a polytheist – and said to him: 'O Abū Umayyah, lend us your weapons so that we can face our enemy tomorrow with their help.' Ṣafwān asked: 'O Muḥammad, do you want to confiscate them?' He said: 'No, I want them temporarily with their return guaranteed till we bring them to you.' He said: 'There is no harm in (doing) this.' So he gave him one hundred coats of arms with the accompanying weapons. They also claim that the Messenger of Allah requested him to transport them too, which he did.[7]

In this case the Prophet borrowed in kind from a non-Muslim. No coercion was involved nor any kind of compensation. There is, however, a hint that the 'purpose' itself concerns the lender also.

(6) The sixth case is that of borrowing a substantial sum of money from a Muslim individual for financing a major battle:

> Ismā'īl son of Ibrāhīm, son of 'Abdullāh, son of Abū Rabī'ah al-Makhzūmī has reported to us from his father who reported about his grandfather that when the Prophet was to attack Ḥunayn he borrowed thirty or forty thousand from him. He repaid it when he came back. Then the Prophet, told him: 'May Allah bless you with prosperity in your family and your property. The proper recompense for lending is repayment and gratitude.'[8]

In another version of this tradition recorded by al-Nasā'ī,[9] the amount of the loan is a definite forty thousand. The same is true of Aḥmad bin Ḥanbal in his *Musnad*.[10] As regards the source of payment, both versions mention money that accrued to the Prophet subsequently.

The battle of Ḥunayn took place in the eighth year after *Hijrah* immediately after the conquest of Makkah. These were comparatively better days for state finances. The accrual of money referred to in the tradition could have been from the spoils of war consequent to the victory at Ḥunayn.

The above is a clear case of borrowing for defence purposes. It is also evident that the sum paid back equalled the sum borrowed and no extra payment was involved.

(7) The last case is that of 'Abbās, the Prophet's uncle, paying a year's *zakāh* in advance, along with that of the current year. Since this was presumably done at the request of the Prophet,[11] it has been construed as a kind of borrowing. The Prophet significantly used the word *aslafa* for the act, a word normally used for lending.

> Ibn 'Abbās is reported to have said that the Messenger of Allah, sent 'Umar as collector of *Zakāh*. He (Ibn 'Abbās) says 'Abbās was rude to him so he came to the Prophet, and informed him. He (Ibn 'Abbās) says, then the Messenger of Allah, told him: ' 'Abbās has advanced to us this year's *Zakāh* of his wealth as well as that of the coming year.'[12]

In summary, the following can be noted.

The Prophet borrowed both in cash and kind, in small amounts as well as large, from Muslims as well as non-Muslims, from men as well as women. The purpose of borrowing was need fulfilment or defence/*jihād*. But he also borrowed to pay off more urgent debts. No coercion was involved in his borrowing. Nor was there any stipulation about repaying more than what was received as the loan. He borrowed when he did not possess, in cash or kind, what could meet the purpose in view. He borrowed in anticipation of future income from which repayment could be made, but he also borrowed when no definite future income was in sight. He always repaid the debts he incurred.

To put the above in proper perspective it should be noted that the usual sources of revenue for meeting public expenditure during the Prophet's time were the following:

(a) *Zakāh* (including *'ushr*) which gradually grew in volume after the second year after *Hijrah* when it was introduced.
(b) *Fay'*, including the produce share from Khaybar which was a steady source of revenue.
(c) Spoils of war out of which a share accrued to the public treasury.
(d) Voluntary donations, often in response to an appeal from the Prophet.

The first three sources brought in nothing during the Prophet's first year in Madīnah, hence exclusive reliance must have been placed on the last. In the light of available reports, revenue from all these sources was meagre till the seventh year when Khaybar was subdued. Some cases of small borrowing for need fulfilment seem to belong to this period. But, as we have noted above, the two cases of substantial borrowing (cases 5 and 6) belong to the post-Khaybar period and relate to defence purposes.

These records of the Prophet's borrowing for public purposes do not mention any attempt by him to appeal for donations before resorting to borrowing, though the lack of reports to this effect does not eliminate the possibility.

Public Borrowing in the Period After the Prophet

We could not find a single instance of public borrowing during the reign of the *Khulafā' al-Rāshidūn* (Pious Caliphs), i.e. during the years 11–40 AH. This is not surprising as revenues from *zakāh* including *'ushr, fay'* including *kharāj,* as well as the spoils of war were steadily rising throughout this period. These revenues would have been sufficient to meet all public expenditure including need fulfilment and *jihād*/defence.

Something similar applies to the next hundred years of Umayyad rule (41–132 AH/661–749 CE). We could not find any instance of state borrowing at the level of central administration. However, there are reports from the provinces of army commanders borrowing to equip their forces or governors borrowing to pay *'aṭāyā* (salaries/pensions) on time, or in order to provide famine-relief. Four specific cases may be noted.

(1) In the first case, an army commander borrowed from traders to buy provisions for a twelve thousand-strong army.[13] He paid them back after some weeks.[14]

The incident belongs, probably, to 65 AH/684 CE. The commander concerned was a *tābi'ī* (i.e. one who has met a Companion of the Prophet), Muhallab bin Abū Sufrah, who died in 83 AH. He was asked by the governorate at Baṣra[15] to take care of the *khārijī* rebellion which dominated Persia and threatened parts of Iraq.

> They took stock of the public treasury and discovered that it had only two hundred thousand dirhams. This was insufficient. Muhallab then sent for the traders and told them: 'For a whole year your business is depressed because the supplies from Ahwāz and Persia have been cut off from you. Let us have some transactions. Then you come with me and I will, God willing, fulfil all my obligations toward you.' They sold to him and he took whatever he needed to equip his army and to provide for it . . . .[16]

This was a case of purchase on credit on a very large scale. Even though no extra returns were involved the traders had a big stake in the arrangement as the success of Muhallab's mission would eventually restore their supplies from Persia.

It is not difficult to imagine that such 'borrowing' or purchase on credit would have been repeated elsewhere too, though not necessarily at central government level.

The report underlines an important point not any less relevant in our age than it was in the seventh century: sometimes it is possible to meet a deficit by purchasing what you need on credit.

In 77 AH, in a similar situation, a man asked by the governor of Khurāsān to launch an attack 'across the river' on Central Asia, is reported to have borrowed from traders and other people in the town of Sughd.[17]

(2) Another case of a provincial officer borrowing for public purposes occurred during the reign of 'Umar bin 'Abd al-'Azīz (99–101 AH/715–17 CE). The officer, Ḥayyān bin Shurayḥ, borrowed the sum of twenty thousand dinars from one Ḥārith bin Thābit to meet a deficit in payments to those registered (*ahl al-Dīwān*). He wrote to the *Amīr al-Mu'minīn* requesting him to arrange repayment to the lender.[18]

(3) Earlier, most probably during 58–59 AH, Sa'īd bin al-'Āṣ (d. 59 AH) the governor of Madīnah during the reign of Mu'āwiyah (41–60 AH/661–80 CE) borrowed to feed people during a famine, having first exhausted all the funds in the public treasury.[19]

(4) The first century of 'Abbāsid rule, from 132 AH to 232 AH was blessed by firm central administration and robust finances. This was followed by a period of weak rulers, domination of Turkish army chiefs and gross financial mismanagement. The Caliphs ruled only nominally as power was exercised by the army commanders while the finances were managed by *wazīrs*. The chief interest of the Caliph was in the huge sums of money flowing into his private treasury (*Bayt al-Māl al-Khāṣṣah*) thanks to the appropriation of lands in the past and the customary gifts presented to the Caliph, especially by the aspirants to public office. It was not unusual, during this period, for the public treasury to be empty while royalty wallowed in money. Often the army did not get paid on time and long delays in the payment of salaries led to protests from the infantry which sometimes culminated in riots in the capital city, Baghdad.

The first reports of public borrowing in our sources appear during the reign of the eighteenth 'Abbāsid Caliph al-Muqtadir who ruled from 295–320 AH (908–32 CE). Al-Muqtadir ascended the throne at the age of thirteen. Real power was wielded by his mother and the *wazīrs* who were changed very frequently. As we shall see below, the urgent need to pay the army while the state coffers were empty was behind most of the public borrowing that occurred.

The nine reports relating to public borrowing given below all pertain to the period 300–33 AH. This period encompasses the rule of four 'Abbāsid Caliphs: al-Muqtadir (295–320 AH), al-Qāhir (320–22 AH), al-Rāḍī (322–29 AH) and al-Muttaqī (329–33 AH). We could not cover the later period for many reasons, not least among them that by then the world of Islam was divided into a dozen units having separate rulers and independent finances. Any study covering only the nominal 'Abbāsid caliphate with its seat in Baghdad would no longer be credible.

It also deserves mention that we have relied on sources almost contemporary to the events being reported, e.g. al-Ṣūlī (d. 335 AH), al-Tanūkhī (d. 384 AH), al-Miskawayh (d. 421 AH) and al-Ṣābī (d. 448 AH). One of the greatest of the early historians of Islam, al-Ṭabarī (d. 310 AH) did not report any case of public borrowing. Later historians drew upon these and other early sources.

Public Borrowing in the Early Fourth Century AH

(1) 'Alī bin 'Īsā[20] used to borrow from traders when some payment came due and he had no other means to make it. He borrowed on the basis of letters of credit (*safātij*) coming from the provinces but not yet due for payment. (He borrowed) ten thousand dinars against payment of a profit of one and a half *dāniq*[21] of silver for each dinar. Every month he owed two thousand and five hundred dirhams as profit.[22] This practice continued with Yūsuf bin Finkhāṣ and Hārūn bin 'Imrān, or their deputies, for sixteen years, and till after their death. They were not turned away till their death. They had gained this position (of state bankers) during the *wazirate* of 'Ubaidullāh bin Yaḥyā bin Khāqān.[23] The ruler did not consider it wise to turn them away so that the *jahbadhah* retained its credibility among the traders and the traders would lend the *jahbadh* in time of need. If the bankers were to be turned away and others[24] were given that position and the traders refused to deal with these, the affairs of the Caliphs would collapse.[25]

(2) Al-Tanūkhī's above statement follows his narration of an incident which culminated in the *wazīr*, 'Ali bin 'Īsā making

a special arrangement with the two bankers named above. He is reported to have told them:

> Every lunar month I need a sum of money to be paid to the infantry troops within the first six days of the month. This amounts to thirty thousand dinars which sometimes is not available to me on the first day of the month, even on the second. I want you two to lend me one hundred and fifty thousand dirhams which you can recover within the month out of the revenues from Ahwāz,[26] because the administration of Ahwāz revenue is already in your charge . . .[27]

Significantly, no 'profits' are promised in this case, nor is there any mention of letters of credit. The author has quoted his source in giving this report whereas the statement quoted earlier is given on his own authority. It is also to be noted that the two bankers named above were Jewish not Muslim.[28]

(3) The two Jewish bankers were given official position by al-Muqtadir's second *wazīr,* Abū'l-Ḥasan 'Alī bin Muḥammad bin al-Furāt[29] whose first occupancy of this office lasted from 296–99 AH.[30] Al-Ṣābī reports one 'Abdullāh Muḥammad bin Ismā'īl al-Anbārī al-Zinjī telling him about this *wazīr*:

> He called Yūsuf bin Finkhāṣ the Jewish *jahbadh,* who was the *jahbadh* of Ahwāz, and told him, 'This situation has arisen and our colleagues have not made the necessary preparations to deal with it. I have assigned their emoluments to (the revenue from) Ahwāz. Now it is very necessary that you pay them in advance for two months. He (Yūsuf bin Finkhāṣ) mentioned the large sums already assigned for advance payment on the Ahwāz account and that it was not possible for him to take on any more demands. He (the *wazīr*) continued to argue with him till he agreed to release one month's pay that very day . . .[31]

(4) Another instance of an interest-bearing loan is cited by Miskawayh. It relates to the *wazīr* Kalwadhānī who held office briefly in 319 AH.

> Ibn Qarābah used to indicate to al-Muqtadir and to Miflaḥ al-Aswad that it was he who helped the affairs of the *wazirate* being performed and that no *wazīr* could do without him. He used to make himself continuously available at Kalwadhānī's place and to lend him, on behalf of Banī al-Barīdī and others, at the profit of one dirham per dinār. He lent him two hundred thousand dinārs which helped the management of Kalwadhānī's affairs . . .[32]

(5) The same person, Ibn Qarābah, is reported to have lent to Ḥusayn bin al-Qāsim, who succeeded Kalwadhānī as *wazīr* in 319 AH, 'at the rate of one dirham per dinār as was his practice'.[33]

(6) Facing a very tight financial situation, Ḥusayn is also reported to have sold some public property to raise five hundred thousand dinārs and to have realized in advance half the money due in 320 AH, some months before the beginning of that year.[34]

(7) After a couple of years, in 323 AH during the reign of Caliph al-Raḍī, we find another *wazīr,* Abū 'Alī bin Muqlah, 'borrowing' from traders who used to supply flour against what was due from Mosul. He raised four hundred thousand dinārs in this manner.[35] Significantly, no 'profits' were involved in this 'borrowing'. However, it becomes clear after a few pages that the 'borrowing' actually amounted to advance payment for grains to be collected from the region as taxes and delivered to traders.[36]

(8) We have yet another report from 323 AH. This time the *wazīr* tried to borrow from traders in order to pay the troops, offering the traders letters of credit (*safātij*). However, the traders disappeared and the effort did not succeed.[37]

(9) Another report by the same author, al-Ṣūlī, also relates to 331 AH. The then *Amīr al-Umarā',* Nāṣir al-Dawlah, upon learning that the money changers were dealing in interest openly, warned them against doing so and obtained their pledges to that effect. According to al-Ṣulī, however, this helped restrain them only a little.[38]

This last report does not concern public borrowing. We have

noted it only to underline the fact that despite the practice of interest-based lending in the market, the authorities remained committed to its elimination till the end of the period we have studied in this paper.

It is difficult to deny, however, that interest was involved in some cases of public borrowing. This reflects the gross mismanagement of the financial affairs of an otherwise prosperous regime as well as the compelling circumstances created by the maintenance of a large force of mercenaries in the capital city Baghdad. The most surprising case of borrowing on interest relates to the *wazīr* 'Alī bin 'Īsā, 'probably the first to obtain a loan by paying interest according to some scholars.'[39] 'Alī bin 'Īsā is reputed to have been a pious Muslim, well versed in *Sharī'ah* sciences and possessing extraordinary managerial skills.[40] The only direct report of this *wazīr* borrowing from bankers is found in al-Tanūkhī and that too does not mention interest (case 2 above). But the same author reports 'Alī bin 'Īsā borrowing regularly with interest on the basis of letters of credit, without quoting any specific source. Even if we accept this sweeping generalization, not corroborated by other historians, the question remains: Did he, under compelling circumstances, deliberately violate the prohibition of interest, or did he look differently at using letters of credit the way he did according to the second report quoted above?

On the basis of the scanty material available, we can distinguish between four types of public borrowing in the early fourth century after *Hijrah*:

1. Advance payment realized in a *salam*-type transaction, i.e. cash obtained against food grains to be delivered in future (Case 7).
2. Discounting letters of credit or bills of exchange, i.e. obtaining cash by surrendering the right to receive a larger amount of cash later (Cases 1 and 8).
3. Cash obtained by promising to pay later with an addition of a percentage of the sum borrowed (Cases 4 and 5).
4. Cash obtained by allowing the lender to recover the sum borrowed from revenue due in the near future (Cases 2 and 3).

As regards case 8 noted above, it is not clear from the report whether it belongs to category 2 or 4.

In all the above cases it was not the Caliph who borrowed, but the *wazīr,* who actually ran the administration. Most of the borrowing was in cash to pay the army on time, but sometimes it was to make some other payments. Public borrowing in this period was largely in the nature of bridge-financing, to be repaid from sure sources of revenue in the near future. Loans were repaid out of the *kharāj* revenue (or land taxes). The lenders were Jewish bankers as well as Muslim traders. The amounts involved were large, but not out of proportion to the state revenues of those times.

One significant point to note is the absence of any reference to need fulfilment as the reason for public borrowing.

As regards the use of coercion in borrowing, we have no clear evidence, even though the sources abound in reports of confiscation of the properties of high officials once they fell from favour and of all kinds of extortions from traders.

It is very difficult to ascertain whether there were any alternatives to public borrowing in so far as it was resorted to. Apparently all other means were exhausted before doing so. Alī bin ʻĪsā is especially reported to have curtailed public expenditure to a very great extent, along with abolishing many extra-*Sharī'ah* taxes.[41]

What circumstances forced a pious man and efficient financial manager, who curtailed public expenditure in an otherwise wasteful affluent society, to borrow at interest, and how he justified it to his own conscience, remains an enigma – at least until further details are available. This deviation from clearly-defined *Sharī'ah* rules seems, however, to be the result of a culmination of many other deviations in the financial management of the state, details of which fill the pages of history books.

Summary and Conclusion

The records of public borrowing examined in this brief study present an interesting contrast. On the one hand, we have the most responsible of rulers borrowing for need fulfilment and *jihād*/defence even when no future revenues were immediately in sight. On the other hand, the records show irresponsible regimes in an age of affluence forced to borrow for bridge-financing, even if they had to violate the prohibition of interest. The strongly worded indictment of public borrowing by jurists like Imām al-Ḥaramayn al-Juwaynī[42] (419–78 AH) is largely in response to the sorry state of affairs that the ʿAbbāsids had reached in the fourth century AH. Given fiscal responsibility and adherence to the *maqāṣid al-Sharīʿah* a different view is more convincing. Much further research is needed to trace the history of public borrowing in the thousand years that separate us from the period studied in this paper. Any guidelines for contemporary policy-making will be better drawn after such research, even though the decisive factors should be the contemporary situation and the example of the Prophet and his Companions.

Meanwhile we can draw some lessons of contemporary relevance from this study:

1. Borrowing, when there is a need, is a legitimate activity even if it is from non-Muslims.
2. Fulfilling needs is one genuine reason justifying borrowing, while *jihād* is another.
3. While early history does not present any record of borrowing for financing economic development, it does provide an indirect justification of the same in an age in which economic development (especially of Third World countries) has become a *sine qua non* for need fulfilment as well as for defence/*jihād*.
4. Since the lender receives no worldly return, public borrowing presumes the lender being motivated by moral and religious considerations. Projects directly related to *jihād*, those directed at feeding, clothing and housing the poor and providing medical care to those who cannot buy the same, as well as educational and moral-spiritual orientation programmes are most likely to motivate people to give *qarḍ ḥasan*. The social authority should, therefore, make public borrowing specific and select purposes most likely to motivate lenders, in order to succeed in mobilizing interest-free loans to the government.
5. The state must repay what it borrows even if to do so necessitates further borrowing.

Notes

1. This and other words in parentheses have been added to clarify the meaning. They are not part of the text.

2. Abū Dāwūd, Tradition No. 3055, *Kitāb al-Imārah, Bāb al-Imām Yaqbil Hadāyā al-Mushrikīn.*

3. Al-Bayhaqī, *Kitāb al-Taflīs, Bāb mā jā'a fī'l-taqāḍī,* Vol. 6, p. 52.

4. Ibn Mājah, Tradition No. 3326, *Kitāb al-Ṣadaqāt, Bāb li-Ṣāḥib al-Ḥaqq maqāl.*

5. Muslim, Tradition No. 114, *Kitāb al-Musāqāt,* Vol. 4, p. 119.

6. Al-'Asqalānī, Vol. 5, p. 57.

7. Ibn Hishām, Vol. 4, p. 68.

8. Ibn Mājah, *Ḥadīth* No. 3424, *Kitāb al-Ṣadaqāt, Bāb Ḥusn al-Qaḍā'.*

9. Al-Nasā'ī, Chapter 44, *Ḥadīth* No. 97, *Kitāb al-Buyū', Bāb al-Istiqrāḍ.*

10. Aḥmad bin Ḥanbal, Vol. 3, p. 305.

11. Al-Bayhaqī, Vol. 4, p. 111.

12. Al-Darāquṭnī, Vol. 2, p. 124.

13. Al-Mubarrad, Vol. 3, p. 1060.

14. *Ibid.,* Vol. 3, p. 1062.

15. Muhallab himself was later appointed Governor of al-Ahwāz by the Umayyad Caliph 'Abd al-Malik bin Marwān (65–76 AH). See al-Mubarrad, Vol. 3, p. 1102.

16. Al-Mubarrad, Vol. 3, p. 1060.

17. Al-Ṭabarī, *Ta'rīkh,* Vol. 6, pp. 312–13.

18. Al-Maqrīzī, *Kitāb al-Khiṭaṭ,* Vol. 1, p. 139.

19. Ibn Manẓūr, *Mukhtaṣar Ta'rīkh Dimashq li-Ibn 'Asākir,* Vol. 9, p. 135.

20. 'Alī bin 'Īsā was first appointed *wazīr* by al-Muqtadir in 301 AH. Later dismissed and imprisoned, he was called upon to shoulder the responsibility again during 315–16 AH. Before his death in 334 AH he was appointed *wazīr* for a third time in 329 AH during the reign of al-Muttaqī. The above report relates to the first period of his *wizārah.*

21. One *dāniq* equalled a sixth of a dirham. A dinār was equal to 15 dirhams.

22. This means that the above rate was a monthly rate amounting to 20% per annum.

23. 'Ubaydullāh bin Khāqān was appointed in 299 AH.

24. The *jahbadh* was originally 'a Financial Clerk, expert in matters of coins, skilled money examiner, treasury receiver, government cashier, money changer or collector . . . . In the time of the 'Abbāsid Caliph al-Muqtadir (295–320 AH/908–32 CE) however, the *jahbadh* emerged as a banker in the modern sense . . .' *Encyclopaedia of Islam,* New edition, Vol. II, p. 382. *Jahbadhah,* therefore, was the banking department of the government.

25. Al-Tanūkhī, Vol. 8, pp. 31–2.

26. A province in Persia.

27. Al-Tanūkhī, Vol. 8, p. 31.

28. Arīb bin Sa'd al-Qurṭubī, p. 77.

29. Al-Tanūkhī, Vol. 8, p. 38.

30. He was succeeded as *wazīr* by 'Ubaydullāh bin Yaḥyā bin Khāqān mentioned in the first report above.

31. Al-Ṣābi', p. 198.

32. Miskawayh, p. 213.

33. *Ibid.,* p. 220.

34. *Ibid.,* p. 226.

35. *Ibid.,* p. 326.

36. *Ibid.,* p. 220.

37. Al-Ṣūlī *Akhbār al-Rāḍī wa'l-Muttaqī min Kitāb al-Awrāq*, p. 76.

38. *Ibid.,* p. 231.

39. W.J. Fischel, *Jews in the Economic and Political Life of Medieval Islam*, p. 25, f.n. 2.

40. See for example, Miskawayh, p. 28; al-Ṣābi', p. 306; Ibn al-Tiqtaqā, p. 241; and Kurd 'Ali, pp. 182–3.

41. See Miskawayh, pp. 27–8, 152; al-Ṣābi', pp. 306, 368; al-Hamadhānī, p. 203.

42. Al-Juwaynī, pp. 274–7.

CHAPTER FOUR

International Economic Relations in Islam

Introduction

This chapter studies the framework for relations between human beings provided by the Islamic world-view of *tawḥīd* and man's vicegerency. Since the grouping of men into nations is a matter of convenience, international relations should also be infused with the spirit of universal brotherhood and mutual support. International economic relations should serve the goals of need fulfilment and progress with freedom from tyranny. They should secure maximum cooperation for the realization of human welfare at the global level, while giving due weight to national and regional preferences. The objective of international economic policies of Islamic nations should be a just and equitable world order most conducive to the choice by individuals and nations of the way of living willed by Allah, which would ensure success in this life as well as in the Hereafter.

The chapter is divided into four sections:

Section One notes some relevant texts from the Qur'ān and the *Sunnah* expounding the Islamic world-view and emphasizing the basic values of equality, brotherhood, cooperation, justice and benevolence. Islam's mission is noted as the guiding force in international relations. The section concludes with three major objectives of external economic policy.

Section Two lists some of the *Sharī'ah* rules governing economic transactions. It also notes some Islamic legal maxims relevant to the conduct of international economic relations. Given the observance of these rules and maxims, freedom of trade and movement should be the normal policy. Restrictions should be applied only when necessary in view of public interest and with a view to realizing the Islamic objectives of justice and equity, the section concludes.

Section Three examines the major policy issues arising in a nation's pursuit of its economic interests, e.g. trade policy, emigration and immigration, capital movements, international monetary relations and developmental strategies in the international perspective. The section discusses the present situation in which the Islamic countries, along with other developing countries, are reduced to a position of economic dependence and backwardness from which they find it difficult to extricate themselves. Part of the responsibility for this is due to the economic policies of the advanced industrialized countries. This situation makes it impossible for these countries to adopt free trade policies. There is no alternative to the Islamic countries coming together and, in cooperation with other developing countries, adopting trade policies and development strategies designed to break the present deadlock.

Section Four focuses on international economic relations in the context of the humanitarian and moral mission of the Muslim *ummah.* Promotion of human rights across the globe, special attention towards the Muslim minorities and greater economic integration among the Islamic nations are some of the essential dimensions of the mission whose implications are traced in this section. In conclusion, it is observed that the *ummah* has to re-order its internal organization and its external relations before it can perform its mission effectively.

Islam's Universal Approach

All human beings constitute a single brotherhood which enjoys a certain dignity and also some superiority over the rest of God's creation.

> Now, indeed, we have conferred dignity on the children of Adam, and borne them over land and sea, and provided them with sustenance out of the good things of life, and favoured them above most of Our creation (17: 70).[1]

> Verily, this Brotherhood of yours is a single Brotherhood, and I am your Lord and Cherisher: therefore serve Me (and no other) (21: 92).[2]

The Prophet (peace be upon him) has affirmed the same by saying:

> I am witness to the fact that all servants (of Allah) are brethren (to one another).[3]

He has exhorted the believers to treat all men equally, caring for their good as they care for their own.

'A man does not believe unless he likes for his brother what he likes for himself.'[4]

The earth with all its resources is a common heritage of mankind. Human life with all its endowments, and the differences therein, is in the nature of a test (6: 165, 7: 10).

> Hallowed be He in whose hand all dominion rests, since He has the power to will anything. He who has created death as well as life. So that He might put you to test (and thus show) which of you is best in conduct, and (make you realize that) He alone is almighty, truly forgiving (67: 1–2).

Emphasis on Justice and Fairness

God likes to have order on earth and justice and fairness in human relations. 'Call unto your sustainer humbly, and in the secrecy of your hearts. Verily, we love not those who transgress the bounds of what is right: hence, do not spread corruption on earth after it has been so well ordered. And call unto Him with fear and longing: Verily God's grace is ever near unto doers of good' (7: 55–6).

Covenants should be honoured, conventions followed, rights recognized and aggression shunned. Everyone should willingly concede to everyone else what is his due.

> . . . And be true to every promise, for, verily, (on judgement day) you will be called to account for every promise you made. And give full measure whenever you measure, and weigh with a balance that is true: this will be (for your own) good, and best in the end (17: 34–5).[5]

Justice requires equality of rights and giving full measure to others.[6] All entitlements should be justly recognized and yielded without any discrimination.

> Behold, God bids you to deliver all that you have been entrusted with unto those who are entitled thereto and whenever you judge between people, to judge with justice (4: 58).

God's universe is endowed with balance and equilibrium. Human society needs the same. To attain this, men must learn to live in peace by mutually recognizing each other's rights and giving everyone his due.

> And the skies has He raised high and has devised (for all things) a measure, so that you too (O men) might never transgress the measure (of what is right) weigh, therefore, (your deeds) with equity and cut not the measure short. And the earth has He spread out for all living beings (55: 7–10).

God's purpose in appointing messengers from amongst men is to enable men to live with justice and equity (57: 25). All the above noted principles – brotherhood, shared heritage and shared destiny, fair dealings and mutual recognition of rights, fulfilment of promises and cooperation – are directed towards the establishment of a just and equitable world order. In the later part of this section, we shall focus on some of the *Sharī'ah* rules relating to economic transactions that are designed to realize this objective. But before doing so, we need to consider the nature of the Islamic community whose external economic relations are the subject of this study.

The Muslim *Ummah* and its Mission

Muslims constitute a single *Ummah* (community). The Islamic injunctions studied above are addressed to the individual Muslim as well as to the Muslim community as a whole. The wording of some of these injunctions might give the impression that all Muslims are duty bound to remain united under a single political leadership as they were during the time of the Prophet. But the *Sharī'ah* does not explicitly prohibit multiplicity of political organizations, as long as the law of God, the *Sharī'ah,* remains supreme, for sovereignty belongs to

Allah alone. Even though the modern concept of the sovereign nation state is alien to Islam, a multiplicity of Muslim states is acceptable, provided these states function within the framework of Islamic law.

At present, about two-thirds of the *ummah* is divided into more than fifty nation states, while more than one-third of it live as citizens of other states. Theoretically, if not in reality, they still constitute a single community bound by the law of God. All these Muslim states and Muslim minority groups in other states are addressed by the injunctions above, each duty-bound to live up to them to the best of its capacity, as ordained by Allah.

> So keep your duty to Allah as best you can, and listen, and obey, and spend, that is better for your souls . . . (64: 16).[7]

Each Muslim state individually, as well as the group of Muslim states collectively, are under an obligation to conduct their economic relations with the non-Muslim world, and individual non-Muslim states, in accordance with the above principles. They are, indeed, duty-bound to maintain brotherly relations with one another and cooperate with one another in discharging the universal mission of the *ummah*. Muslim states are obligated to care for the religious freedom, human rights and economic well-being of their Muslim brothers living as minorities in the rest of the world. They are also required to ensure the religious freedom, human rights and economic well-being of their non-Muslim citizens. All this necessarily follows from the supremacy of the *Sharī'ah* in the conduct of a Muslim state and its external relations. The Islamic doctrine of collective duties (*farḍ kifāyah*) makes need fulfilment and protection of every Muslim a collective obligation of the entire *ummah*. Hence, the external economic relations of Muslim states should be conducted in a manner conducive to the recognition by other nations of the just rights of their Muslim subjects and to removing any obstacles in the way of exercising these rights. Muslims living in non-Muslim states, individuals as well as groups, are also duty-bound to deal justly with all, to give every entity its due, to care for the good of their fellow countrymen and to work sincerely for the good of mankind.

The integrating force is common allegiance to the *Sharī'ah* which will make all the constituent parts of the contemporary Muslim community, nation states as well as Muslim minorities, serve in unison the Islamic mission.

The Muslim community is a moral community. It has to conduct itself morally. It is also charged with a mission relating to mankind as a whole.

> You are the best community that has ever been brought forth for (the good of) mankind. You enjoin the doing of what is right and forbid the doing of what is wrong, and you believe in God . . . (3: 110).
>
> . . . and that there might grow out of you a community (of people who invite unto all that is good, and enjoin the doing of what is right and forbid the doing of what is wrong and it is they, they who will attain a happy state (3: 104).
>
> And thus we willed you to be a community of the middle way, so that (with your lives) you might bear witness to the truth before all mankind, and that the Apostle might bear witness to it before you (2: 143).

We can easily identify three distinct, though closely interrelated, items in the global agenda before the *ummah,* as laid down in thc above verses: to exemplify Islam through its own conduct (being witness), to enjoin right and forbid wrong, and to work for the good of mankind (as implied by the Arabic prefix *li* (for) in the first quoted verse and the word *khayr* (good) in the second one). The requirements of the first two items are obvious: the community should never adopt an immoral posture, it must conduct all its affairs, including international economic relations, in accordance with the principles of morality and justice. Working for the good of mankind lays explicit emphasis on what is already implied by a moral stance, i.e. caring for the material well-being of all men and women. The *ummah* cannot be indifferent to poverty, hunger and disease anywhere in the world, just as it cannot ignore tyranny, denial of human rights and persecution on religious grounds. It must care for all men and women: their need fulfilment and their dignity.

This concern of the *ummah* for justice and equity and for

mankind's material well-being is underlined in many Qur'ānic verses and Traditions, which cannot be cited here due to limitations of space. We will note only three traditions from the Prophet which clearly indicate his concern for the material well-being of people living outside his territorial jurisdiction.

Al-Māwardī reports a tradition from the Prophet, narrated by Abū Hurayrah, which says, 'Once bad remarks were made about the non-Arabs before the Prophet. The Prophet advised against doing so and said, "Do not abuse them because they developed the lands of Allah and (as a result) the servants of Allah could live in those lands." '[8]

The Prophet never hesitated to extend material help to people in distress, even when they happened to live across the border. It is reported that once he sent five hundred dinārs to be distributed among the poor of Makkah (before it came under his rule) who were suffering hardship due to famine.[9] During the same period when the supply of wheat from Yamāmah to Makkah was stopped at the behest of an influential chief, Thumāmah, who had recently embraced Islam, the Makkans appealed to the Prophet in the name of kinship and good relations. The Prophet wrote to Thumāmah to persuade him to let them have their supplies as usual.[10]

Objectives of External Economic Policy

It is possible to deduce from the above discussion some policy objectives for the economic relations of a Muslim nation with other nations. These are three:

(i) Preserving and promoting the economic interests of one's own people, priority being given to need fulfilment.[11]

(ii) Observing the *Sharī'ah* rules relating to economic transactions with a view to ensuring justice and equity.

(iii) Strengthening the *ummah* and serving the mission of the Islamic community in cooperation with other Muslim peoples by exemplifying Islam, communicating its message and promoting human welfare at the global level.

The highest priority attaches to the third objective as it defines the *raison d'être* of the *ummah*. Observance of *Sharī'ah* rules and ensuring justice takes precedence over national economic interests which should be promoted within the framework of *Sharī'ah* rules and the Islamic mission.

We discuss these objectives and their implications for international economic relations in the following sections. First, we discuss the *Sharī'ah* rules relevant for the subject under study.

Sharī'ah Rules Governing Economic Transactions

The *Sharī'ah* does not have separate ethical norms for dealing with aliens. Muslims are bound by the same rules of conduct irrespective of the beliefs of those they are dealing with. A brief summary of the *Sharī'ah* rules governing economic transactions is given below. For details one has to consult some of the standard legal compendiums of Islamic law.

All economic transactions require the willingness of the concerned parties with the provision that the goods and services transacted do not belong to the prohibited category and the transaction is free from the following corrupt practices.

1. *Ribā*, i.e. interest on loans and exchange of unequal quantities of similar fungibles. Gold or silver or a particular paper currency must be exchanged in equal quantities. When gold and silver or different paper currencies are exchanged with one another, the quantities can be unequal but the exchange must be simultaneous.
2. *Qimār,* i.e. gambling, bet and wager. The essence of gambling is taking a risk deliberately created or invited, which is not necessary in economic activity, to gain thereby.
3. *Ghaban,* i.e. fraud, especially that relating to the characteristics of a product.
4. *Ikrāh,* i.e. coercion, or imposing a contract, or a condition therein, on an unwilling party.
5. *Bay' al-muḍṭarr,* i.e. exploitation of need, e.g. by charging an exorbitantly high price.

6. *Iḥtikār,* i.e. withholding supplies of essential goods and services with a view to raising prices.
7. *Najsh,* i.e. raising prices by making false bids.
8. *Gharar,* i.e. hazard or uncertainty surrounding a commodity, its quantity, price, time of payment, time of delivery, etc. (with the provision that some little *gharar* can be ignored if it is humanly impossible to eliminate it).
9. *Jahl mufḍī ilā al-nizā',* i.e. such lack of information about a commodity, its quantity, price, etc., as may lead to dispute.

An Islamic nation's trade with the outside world, its commercial policy, its financial transactions with other parties, and its developmental strategies involving transfer of technology, economic aid, borrowing abroad, etc., all must be free from the above-mentioned corrupt practices.

Difficulties may arise, however, in the context of observing some of these rules when the other party is resorting to corrupt practices and harmful policies such as *ribā,* monopoly pricing, price discrimination, dumping or harmful restrictions on movement of people, materials, monies, services and ideas. In such situations, Islamic nations should be allowed to protect their interests through suitable measures including reciprocal restrictions. They may also justifiably resort to joint action directed at ensuring justice and preventing oppression.

Another type of conflict may arise when the realization of a particular national interest (*maṣlaḥah*) involves some damage (*ḍarar*) to another nation. As we shall note below, the jurists have laid down certain general rules to guide the decision-makers in such conflict situations. It should be noted, however, that the temporary disadvantage to a party caused by fair competition among traders does not constitute damage as it eventually serves the public interest (see Article 26 of the *Majallah* quoted below).

There may also arise exceptional situations in which the observance of a particular *Sharī'ah* rule might expose a nation to extreme hardship and unbearable losses. Such a situation has to be resolved by discretionary policies, decided upon by the social authority after due consultations, in the light of certain

Sharīʿah rules of a general nature. Some of these rules are noted below.

The legal maxims noted below are taken from the Ottoman *Majallah.*[12] They represent a wide consensus of jurists and find support in every school of Islamic law. In many specialized works by jurists belonging to different schools of Islamic law they have been substantiated by the text as well as by the spirit of their original sources of Islamic law, the Qur'ān and the *Sunnah.* Some of the maxims deal with harmful effects of actions or damages. They seek to minimize their incidence and give precedence to removal of public damage.

(i) Causing damage[13] and retaliating by damage is not allowed. (19)
(ii) Damage shall be removed. (20)
(iii) A damage shall not be removed by doing a like damage. (25)
(iv) Severe damage may be removed by doing a lighter damage. (27)
(v) A private damage shall be tolerated in order to prevent a public damage.(26)
(vi) A damage shall be removed to the extent possible. (31)

Another set of maxims deal with *maṣāliḥ* and *mafāsid,* i.e. goods and bads, or utilities and disutilities. They help the decision-maker in resolving conflict situations.

(vii) When there is a (unavoidable) choice between two bads,[14] remedy of the greater one is sought by choosing (to do) the smaller one (28)
(viii) (If necessary) the lesser of two evils shall be chosen (29).
(ix) Any action (by the Social Authority) affecting the people shall be in the public interest.[15] (58)
(x) Preventing bads is prior to acquiring goods. (30)

Lastly, we note three maxims dealing with exceptional circumstances:

(xi) Hardship brings about relaxation (17).

(xii) Necessities make lawful what is (normally) prohibited (21).

(xiii) What is permitted out of necessity is limited to the extent necessary (22).

Read together in the context of international economic relations, the two sets of rules cited above are clear in their purpose and intent. These relations should be just and fair and everyone should avoid adopting policies that could be harmful to others. If and when any party adopts harmful policies the aggrieved party has a right to protect its interests and retaliate, but the best policy is to prevent such action through joint action and international agreements. Also, if and when observance of a *Sharī'ah* rule causes extreme hardship to a people, that particular rule may be held in abeyance till a way out is found. This is quite clear in the light of the last three maxims noted above.

Special importance is attached to international agreements. When an Islamic nation, or group of nations, willingly enters into any agreement with non-Muslim nations, they should abide by it and fulfil all obligations arising from it. Presently, Muslim countries are party to a large number of international agreements as members of the United Nations and its subsidiaries. They are also members of the Organization of Islamic Conference (OIC) and some other regional organizations. Unless any of these commitments is, on scrutiny, found to be *ultra vires* of *Sharī'ah* or to have been secured under duress, Islamic nations should meet them fully in the interest of a just world order.

It should also be noted that some of the above-mentioned maxims, e.g. (ii), (iv), (vi) and (x) provide grounds for imposing economic sanctions against erring parties.

We shall now discuss the first of the three policy objectives noted above: How an Islamic nation can preserve and promote the economic interests of its people in matters relating to foreign trade, exchange rates, capital movements, emigration and immigration, economic aid, etc.

Promotion of National Economic Interests

Trade Freedom

God has permitted trade and encouraged mobility for that purpose.

> God has made buying and selling lawful (2: 275).
>
> And when the prayer is ended, disperse freely on the earth and seek to obtain (something) of God's bounty . . . (62: 10).
>
> And He it is Who has made the sea subservient (to His laws), so that you might eat fresh meat from it, and take from it gems which you might wear. And on that (very sea) one sees ships ploughing through the waves, so that you might (be able to) go forth in quest of some of His bounty, and thus have cause to be grateful (to him) (16: 14).

Any restriction on freedom of trade and movement of factors of production would therefore require some justification. Such a justification can come only on the basis of public interest (*maṣlaḥah*). Some of the circumstances justifying restrictions on the basis of national economic interests or on Islamic ideological grounds are noted below. But the basic position remains that of freedom of trade and movement. Men are free to trade what they wish at the prices they wish. They are also free to move when and wherever they like. They are also free to hold their wealth in any form they like and to invest their savings where they like, provided they observe the *Sharī'ah* rules noted above.

What is true of trade and mobility of factors of production is also true of rates of exchange between currencies. They are left to be determined by the market forces of demand and supply, unless there is reason to control them.

The state can intervene only to prevent violation of *Sharī'ah* rules and in order to protect and promote public interest (*maṣlaḥah*). Modern conditions necessitate taking a macroeconomic view of national economic interests. Public interest cannot be protected in an *ad hoc* manner, proceeding case by case. Domestic goals relating to employment, need fulfilment and equitable distribution, and the objective of maintaining a reasonable degree of stability in prices, constitute the essential dimensions of a comprehensive view of public interest.

Since state intervention in order to protect or promote public interest generally involves restraints on individual freedoms, the crucial thing is the mode of decision-making, i.e. who identifies public interest and the measures necessary to protect or promote it. In accordance with the Qur'ānic prescription, 'and whose rule (in all matters of common concern) is consultation among themselves' (42: 38), a decision should be arrived at through consultation at the appropriate level. Such consultation can ensure that the interests of all concerned are taken into consideration without any discrimination. Open discussion of the issues involved, in order to give everyone a chance to be heard, followed by efforts to arrive at a consensus in the relevant consultative body, are necessary for this purpose. In the context of international economic relations, it is mostly the consultative body at national level which will be involved. But in some cases the nature of the issue may call for a decision at some regional or international level to which nations may voluntarily commit themselves.

In the contemporary world, there are a large number of nation states, some grouped together into regional economic blocs, pursuing their diverse economic interests, sometimes with disregard for the similar interests of other nations. The world is dominated by a score of economically-advanced countries whereas more than 130 developing countries lag behind in every respect. Islamic countries mostly belong to the group of poor and weak countries. In the past they followed other developing countries in adopting protectionist policies. These policies failed. But they are fearful of the new openness coming in the wake of economic globalization and GATT. There are difficult choices to be made in the context of transfer of technology, capital movements, multinational corporations and monetary integration. It is not possible to discuss all these problems in this chapter. Moreover, specific policy options have to be exercised in the overall context of development and gaining strength for the Islamic community and decreasing their dependence on non-Muslim nations. Below, we list and briefly review some of the major issues in the perspective of the *Sharī'ah* rules stated above.

Issues in the Pursuit of National Economic Interests

- Restrictions on trade through tariffs, quotas, etc.
- Protection of home industries in any other way.
- Restrictions on the movement of labour, the problem of 'brain drain' and immigration policies.
- Restrictions on capital movements, on investment abroad and on foreign investment in the home country. The issue of integration with the world capital market.
- Restrictions on foreigners owning property and managing enterprises in the home country; the issue of multinationals.
- Allowing foreign equity participation, quasi-equity arrangements, leasing arrangements and other 'new forms of investment'.
- Borrowing abroad and/or lending abroad at public and private levels.
- Allowing multinational banking.
- Intervention in the exchange market and controlling the external value of currency.
- Allowing free convertibility of currency.
- Integration with the world monetary system or insulating the domestic economy through independent management of money.
- Policies relating to employment and price stability in the context of inflationary or deflationary pressures originating in the external sector of the economy.
- Distributive policies and their requirements in relation to taxation of foreigners and foreign assets of citizens, etc.
- Development strategies: export promotion versus import substitution.
- Seeking foreign aid or giving aid to others.
- Transfer of technology.
- The desirability of self-sufficiency in food and other strategic materials: political and ideological reasons for lessening dependence.
- Regional economic integration: economic unions, clearing unions, customs unions, etc.
- Inter-Islamic economic cooperation and its implications for regional and international economic relations. The issue of an Islamic Common Market.
- Multinational commodity agreements and cartelization.

The above list of issues, by no means exhaustive, is formidable indeed. A detailed examination of each issue in the light of *Sharīʻah* rules and the Islamic legal maxims noted above is not possible here. It should be noted, however, that only some of the above issues involve *Sharīʻah* rules governing economic transactions. Most of them involve the calculus of *maṣlaḥah* and *mafsadah* on which the above-mentioned legal maxims throw some light. As one goes down the list of issues, with the actual condition of present-day developing Islamic countries in mind, one feels that a case for free trade policies is not always obvious. There are, for example, important *maṣāliḥ* (public interests) to be protected by regulating capital movements and transfer of technology. But such regulation is becoming less and less possible due to the revolution in information and communication technology. Nations have to reconcile themselves to openness and free trade. The weak have to rely on regional cooperation in confronting the strong. Malaysia and Indonesia may provide some lessons for other Muslim countries. It is not possible, however, to prescribe policies valid for all Islamic countries all the time. Actual choice of policy should be based on the circumstances an Islamic country faces at a particular time.

We will now briefly review some of the above issues, assuming developing Islamic countries face similar circumstances.

Trade Restrictions and Protectionism

Economic theory has identified the 'infant industry argument' as the only valid ground for protection from a world point of view.[16] Protection through appropriate tariffs on the import of relevant goods allows a domestic industry sufficient time to develop and compete with the world industry. In practice, however, vested interests tend to prolong protective measures to the disadvantage of the national economy. It is also argued that a production subsidy coupled with an equal tax on consumption serves the domestic industry better than import restrictions. Protection is also justified when the protected industries are likely to generate 'externalities' from which other home industries are likely to benefit.[17]

Tariffs can be an effective means of improving terms of trade. The terms of trade of the primary goods producing countries have been declining since the beginning of this century.[18] International agreements are needed to protect the interests of the primary goods producing developing countries.

Trade restrictions are justified in retaliation for similar restrictions imposed by the other party. Import duties were first introduced in Islam by Caliph 'Umar when Muslim traders complained to him that other countries were collecting duties from them at the entry points to those countries.[19] If other countries do not impose any duties the Muslim country is also advised not to impose any duty.[20] But economic theory has warned of the 'beggar thy neighbour' consequences of such policies, a point which should receive due consideration in the calculus of *maṣlaḥah* and *mafsadah* in any particular case. Free trade policies can flourish only as a result of international agreements which provide sufficient incentives to those countries which see an advantage in protectionist policies.[21] This is precisely what GATT tried to achieve and what the World Trade Organization is supposed to ensure.

Restrictions on the Movement of People

Restrictions on citizens of other countries taking jobs in the home country are on the ground of the unemployment existing in the home country. Since existing differences in skill levels have historical roots and cannot be removed in the short run, these restrictions may be justified in view of the ultimate responsibility of the state to provide jobs and to take care of the needs of its citizens when they are unemployed.

Restrictions on skilled manpower moving abroad to take jobs (brain drain) may be justified on the ground of national needs, inability of the country to pay wages comparable to those in the world market[22] and the fact that national resources have been invested in creating those skills.

The first argument loses its relevance if there is a labour shortage at home. The second argument collapses if suitable jobs for highly qualified people are not available at home. Entry of foreign labour may raise productivity at home and pressurize domestic labour to improve its skills. Remittances from nationals working abroad have been a significant source of foreign exchange for many developing countries in the last two decades. In any case, the cure for the brain drain is adequate manpower planning and not restrictions on mobility which are also difficult to impose.

We can, therefore, conclude that the economic arguments for restrictions on the mobility of labour and professionals are at best temporary in nature. Freedom of movement is a fundamental right of every individual and the world as a whole stands to gain by it.

This leaves out the cultural ground for restricting the movement of people into and out of an Islamic country. An Islamic society with a good standard of commitment need not restrict such movements as they have historically been a means of spreading Islam.

Any restrictions placed on the entry of a Muslim individual into a Muslim country can be justified only on economic grounds, if at all. Seen in the context of the desirability of greater economic integration among Islamic countries, economic measures for restricting the movement of Muslims within the world of Islam can, at best, be of a short-term nature.

Capital Movement

Should individuals be free to invest their savings in other countries and to own assets located abroad? Should foreigners be allowed to invest in a Muslim country, own property, run factories, etc.? Should it make a difference if the foreigner is a Muslim? Should capital funds be allowed to move freely across borders in search of maximum profits – and security? Economic theory has generally supported the case of freedom in all these respects, but the practice in almost all developing countries is that of strict regulation and control. Muslim nation states, too, do not relax any of these rules in favour of Muslims.

The developing countries' fear of flight of capital and dominance by foreigners, which is responsible for the abovementioned restrictions, is not entirely unjustified. Automatic functioning of the world capital markets is perceived to benefit the stronger, larger and better informed parties – all located in the advanced countries – to the disadvantage of the weak, poor and capital-starved developing countries who can offer neither security nor stability. The state steps in, therefore, to manage the capital market and regulate the role of foreigners in the interest of capital formation at home. Foreign investment by nationals is generally not allowed. Foreign private capital is welcome in some countries, but others prefer official aid. Multinationals are allowed but with conditions relating to local participation and transfer of technology. Other regulations abound, but the more there are the more they tend to favour a small section of businessmen, making life more difficult for the rest. If the purpose of these regulations is to keep investment policies in line with national priorities, it should be clearly laid down and then foreign investors should be allowed to enter the domestic market. It would also serve the interest of the Muslim countries to create conditions favourable for greater mobility of capital within the group of Muslim countries. Lack of such conditions has been the major cause in Muslim countries of capital's flight to the West. Most developing countries have relaxed these regulations to their advantage.

But some regulation of the capital market in Islamic countries is also necessary to keep it free from interest, gambling and other corrupt practices. Special attention has to be paid to speculative movement of funds which, as Keynes remarked half a century ago, 'threaten disorganizing all steady business'.[23]

Foreign private capital should be welcome in Islamic countries on a profit-sharing basis. A host of new forms of investment are available which do not involve interest or any of the corrupt practices noted earlier. Leasing also provides a secure basis for acquiring capital equipment from abroad. Prohibition of interest in effect removes lending and borrowing as the basis of capital movements, so far as Islamic countries are concerned. A Muslim nation should neither lend nor borrow on interest. But loans without interest can still have a role in multinational banking as well as in transactions between central banks.

Economic aid in the form of interest-free loans may also assume greater proportions given increased cooperation between Muslim countries.

It is only in extreme need and under exceptional circumstances that a Muslim nation may invoke the last-mentioned legal maxims noted above to justify, temporarily, interest-based borrowing from other nations, foreign commercial banks or international financial agencies. The issue of outstanding foreign debts apart, Muslim nations should strive to do away with foreign borrowing in future by switching to profit-sharing and leasing arrangements with their creditors. To the extent it is not possible to do so they have no option but to cut their (public) expenditures and rely on increased inter-Islamic cooperation for meeting their financial needs. Removal of impediments to the inflow of private business investment from outside can also help a lot.

International Monetary Relations

What kind of a monetary system can we envisage for a contemporary Muslim country? Should it be an automatically functioning system with no restrictions on convertibility of currency, no control of exchange rates, no curbs on multinational banking and full integration with the international monetary system? Or, should it be a system of managed money with limited facilities for convertibility, a controlled exchange rate and a regulated banking sector, so that the authorities have effective control of the domestic money supply? It is the latter scenario which obtains in almost all contemporary Muslim countries. The reasons are easy to see. The world monetary system is presently in a chaotic state. The collapse of the Bretton Woods system and the freely-floating dollar has removed any semblance of an international monetary system and no agreement is in sight for instituting a new world monetary order. The suggestion of a return to gold as the basis of money, both domestic and international, is ill-conceived as the so-called gold standard never really provided a fully automatic monetary system.[24] In any case, gold cannot meet the expanding needs of mankind for a medium of exchange and an international reserve. The idea of a world central bank with a fiat money acceptable to all nations is also not acceptable as it simply transfers the difficult task of managing money from the national authorities to an international authority. Such a centralized management would be an impossible task in view of the diverse interests of individual nations.[25]

Till such time as mankind can envision a world monetary system acceptable to all nations, rich as well as poor, strong as well as weak, there is no alternative to nationally managed monies supplemented by regional and international cooperative arrangements directed at specific ends such as orderly changes in exchange rates, easy supply of international credit and efficient clearance of claims, etc.

It is realistic to assume that central banks and national governments can no longer exercise tight control on exchange rates and domestic money supplies except at a high cost in terms of production and employment. No modern economy can simultaneously ensure domestic price stability, full employment and a stable external value of its home currency.[26] Differential rates of productivity changes in the countries of the world and changing expectations make it an impossible task. The order of priorities and acceptable degrees of trade off between the three objectives cannot be the same for all countries. It depends on the position of a country in the world economy, the relative size of its external sector and the extent of unemployment in the economy.

Freely-floating exchange rates damage the interests of developing countries which are obliged to import more than they export. Their task is made more difficult by the resulting uncertainties in the capital market. They need a regime of fixed exchange rates to plan their development. Expansion of trade between themselves and dealing with the developed countries as a group through their own institutions may decrease uncertainties and lessen their need for international reserve currencies.

In a free economy with a relatively small external sector, domestic stability should take precedence over exchange rate stability. If the external sector dominates then the exchange rate becomes more important. Full employment policies and welfare services cannot be maintained with declining real production and shrinking international trade. Inflation is sure to frustrate these policies sooner or later. Islamic countries will understandably be under popular pressure to guarantee job opportunities and need fulfilment. But experience of the developing countries during the last four decades has proved that these objectives cannot be realized through deficit financing. Expanding real production through higher productivity and larger international trade is necessary for that purpose. This leads us to the issue of development strategies which we proceed to examine in the context of international economic relations.

Development Strategies in the International Perspective

The dual economy approach – a small urban capitalist sector geared to the world economy in the hope that it will pull along the remaining backward sectors – has failed miserably. In any case, it does not suit the egalitarian and participatory temper of an Islamic economy. National development should mobilize the entire population, urban as well as rural, through assuring everyone – the peasant, the wage labour, the entrepreneur and the capital owner – that the fruits of their contributions to the national product will flow back to them in good measure. The normal material incentives to work, save and invest need also to be buttressed by the Islamic mission. Corruption should be eliminated and a truly consultative political process should restore the trust of the populace in decision-making at national level.

In the international context, the unsuccessful experience of many developing countries with a policy of import substitution has led to a preference for export promotion as the best strategy. Sometimes the efforts of the developing countries in this regard are frustrated because of the refusal of the advanced countries to let their product in. Developing countries are no longer content to be producers of primary commodities because of the deteriorating terms of trade for these commodities. The impasse can only be broken through international agreements since the capacity of primary goods' producers to dictate their will through cartelization is very limited and, at best, transitory. These countries have to diversify into the production of manufactures. This would require group action designed to enlarge the market and ensure greater specialization within the group so that economies of large-scale production can be enjoyed.

Often in international economic relations a situation arises in which the good of all can best be realized by generally agreed fair arrangements. But such an arrangement fails to materialize because individual nations, or groups of nations, find themselves in a position to secure larger gains through a different policy. There is no alternative, however, to working patiently for universally-acceptable fair arrangements, especially in view of the fact that the perception of what is fair differs from nation to nation, and from group to group. Islamic developing countries have to make the best of GATT and WTO and improve their competitive advantages in the global economy.

There is wide scope for regional economic cooperation among the developing countries. This should apply especially to Muslim countries in North Africa, West Asia and South East Asia forming geographically contiguous regions. Clearance unions and payment unions can help promote inter-Islamic trade. A currency union could be even more helpful. The issue of customs union and eventually an Islamic common market should receive greater attention than they have received so far. We mention them here to underline their importance in the absence of universally-acceptable arrangements in the fields of trade and finance. It would be a good gesture to invite neighbouring developing countries to join these Islamic groupings, unless there are strong political or cultural reasons applying to a particular case. More often than not, cultural considerations can be taken care of in other ways, and what is more conducive to resolving political conflicts than the opportunity of making solid economic gains through mutual cooperation?

Presently, Muslim countries in Africa, West Asia and South East Asia are already members of some regional groupings, besides being members of the OIC and its subsidiaries. There is no essential conflict between greater economic integration between Islamic countries and their participation, along with neighbouring non-Muslim countries, in the respective regional organizations. Their economic problems are similar, and they need a joint strategy in dealing with the dominant advanced industrial countries and for securing just international agreements.

Demands of the *Ummah*'s Mission

We now turn to the third objective of international economic relations in the Islamic perspective, which requires the Muslim peoples to strengthen their mutual bonds to extend material help to other peoples who need help and to popularize Islamic ideas and values among them. Individual Muslim nations, and the group of Muslim nations, can play this role better if they are, economically, in a position to give to others rather than being obliged to take from them. The more they need other peoples' help the less credible their call to Islam becomes. The first requirement of this policy norm is, therefore, for the Islamic nations to minimize their dependence on others.

Some Islamic countries are in a position to spare some resources for the poor developing countries. Even the average ones should make some sacrifice to relieve extreme poverty and suffering elsewhere. They should do so individually as well as collectively through such institutions as the OIC and the Islamic Development Bank. The rich ones should contribute generously to the agencies set up for these purposes.

The existence of sizeable Muslim minorities in many countries of the world assumes special significance in the context of Islamic mission. The highest priority attaches to ensuring human rights and freedom to live in accordance with *Sharī'ah*. This could be done by the Islamic nations maintaining good bilateral relations with these countries and exercising vigilance through the United Nations. The treatment that non-Muslim minorities living in Muslim countries receive is of crucial importance in this context.

Muslim countries should endeavour to extend all possible help to the Muslim minorities to enable them to improve their skills and educational standards. Encouraging Muslim-managed enterprises through participatory finance and favourable treatment of Muslim job seekers from the minority countries could also help improve their economic conditions.

The mission involves much more. Muslim nations have to demonstrate, especially in the conduct of international economic relations, that they care for man's freedom from tyranny and hunger more than they care for national glory and material progress. They should be willing, therefore, to buy peace and freedom *for others* at the cost of some of their own economic interests. Even their alliance with Third World developing countries in order to secure a better deal from the advanced countries, should not deteriorate into an all-out confrontation. Their love and care must encompass all human beings, the West included.

But the fact remains that the *ummah* cannot play its desired role unless it re-orders it internal organization as well as its relations with the rest of the world. In this latter context, its present state of dependence and backwardness can be ended only by planned efforts in cooperation with other developing countries trapped in a similar situation. Free trade or *laissez faire* will not end the domination of the weak by the strong.

Internally, individual Muslim countries are at present linked more closely to the dominant industrial economies than they are to one another, through trade and factor movements. This is not how Islam conceives the relationship of Muslim peoples among themselves. This is against the economic and political interest of the *ummah*. It keeps it weak and vulnerable to cultural, economic and political domination by anti-Islamic and un-Islamic powers. The strength of the *ummah*, its defence against external threats, and the imperative of its taking the position of exemplifying Islam and calling towards it, necessitate if not unification, at least greater integration: social, economic and political.

It is way beyond the scope of this paper to discuss how such a re-ordering can be effected. Greater economic and political integration among the group of Islamic nations is, however, a must in this regard so that the external economic relations of the *ummah* are channelled largely through the group organization at a collective level. This would secure for the group of Islamic countries not only better terms of trade but also save its individual members from the state of total dependence on the developed countries in which many of them find themselves at present. The idea of an Islamic common market deserves special attention in this regard. It would provide a market large enough for realizing gains from free trade by way of specialization and large-scale economies. An Islamic common market would, however, have to be so designed that these gains were shared equitably by the poor and rich members. Special arrangements would also be needed to enlist the cooperation of other developing countries, especially those neighbouring Islamic countries in Africa and Asia. As noted earlier, there are several regional groupings comprising Islamic and non-Islamic developing countries. An Islamic common market would need to accommodate existing arrangements unless ideological and cultural considerations necessitated some modifications.

Conclusion

In conclusion, we must re-emphasize the universality of the Islamic approach to international economic relations. Islam emphasizes brotherhood and cooperation, justice and fair dealing. The Muslim *ummah* must order its internal and external economic policies in accordance with the *Sharī'ah* and stand united in calling towards and exemplifying Islam. Islam favours trade freedom and restrictions on the movements of people do not fit its universal approach. But, for the time being, domination of the world economic scene by a score of advanced industrial countries makes it imperative for developing Islamic countries, along with other developing countries to take special measures to improve their competitive capabilities and protect their vital interests. The *ummah* should, however, focus on its humanitarian and ideological mission and regard economic strength as a necessary means to achieve that end.

Notes

1. The numbers in parentheses refer to the Chapter (*Sūrah*) of the Qur'ān followed by the number of the verse. All translations are, unless otherwise specified, taken from Muhammad Asad, *The Message of the Qur'ān* (Gibraltar, Dār al-Andalus, 1980).

2. Abdullāh Yusuf Ali, *The Holy Qur'ān, Text, Translation and Commentary* (Leicester, The Islamic Foundation, 1978). Also see 49: 13.

3. Abū Dāwūd, *Sunan, Kitāb al-Ṣalāt, Bāb mā yaqūl al-rajul idhā sallam.*

4. Al-Bukhārī, *Ṣaḥīḥ, Bāb min al-īmān an yuḥibba li-Akhīh . . .*

5. Also see 16: 90–3.

6. See 11: 84, 85.

7. M.M. Pickthall, *The Glorious Qur'ān* (Makkah, The Muslim World League, 1977).

8. Al-Māwardī, *Ādāb al-Dīn wa'l-Dunyā* (Beirut, Dār Iḥyā' al-Turāth al-'Arabī, 1979), p. 115.

9. Al-Sarakhsī, *al-Mabsūṭ,* Vol. 10 (Beirut, n.d.), p. 92; also, al-Sarakhsī, *Sharḥ Kitāb al-siyar al-Kabīr li-Muḥammad bin al-Ḥasan al-Shaybānī,* Vol. 1, ed. Salāḥ al-Dīn al-Munajjid (Cairo, 1971), p. 96.

10. Ibn Hishām, *Sīrat al-Nabī,* Vol. 4 (Beirut, Dār al-Fikr, n.d.), p. 316; also al-'Asqalānī, *Fatḥ al-Bārī Sharḥ Saḥīḥ al-Bukhārī,* Vol. 8 (Beirut, Dār al-Ma'rifah, n.d.), p. 88.

11. The theoretical background for this objective has been discussed in Chapters One and Two above.

12. Compiled between 1869 and 1876. For Arabic text with commentary, see 'Alī Ḥaydar, *Durar al-Ḥukkām Sharḥ Majallat al-Aḥkām,* 2 Vols. (Beirut, n.d.). For an English translation see C.R. Tyser, *The Majelle* (Lahore, Law Publishing Company, 1980). The numbers in parentheses that follow the texts quoted below correspond to the numbers of the clauses in the *Majallah.*

13. Arabic: *ḍarar.*

14. Arabic: *mafsadah.*

15. Arabic: *maṣlaḥah.*

16. C.P. Kindleberger, *International Economics* (Homewood, Ill, Richard D. Irwin Inc., 1968), p. 128.

17. Paul R. Krugman, 'Is Free Trade Passe?', *Economic Perspectives,* Vol. 1, No. 2 (Fall 1987), pp. 137–8.

18. Enoz R. Grilli and Maw Chung Yang, 'Primary Commodity Prices and the Terms of Trade of Developing Countries: What the Long Run Shows', *The World Bank Economic Review,* Vol. 2, No. 1 (Jan. 1988), pp. 1–47.

19. Abū Yūsuf, *Kitāb al-Kharāj* (Cairo, Dār al-Iṣlāḥ, 1981), pp. 275–6, No. 299; Abū 'Ubayd, *Kitāb al-Amwāl* (Beirut, Dār al-Fikr, 1975), p. 635, No. 1636 and p. 638, No. 1653.

20. Majid Khadduri, *The Islamic Law of Nations, Shaybānī's Siyar* (Baltimore, Maryland, Johns Hopkins University Press, 1966), pp. 174–5.

21. Harry G. Johnson, *International Trade and Economic Growth* (Cambridge, Mass, 1967), p. 55.

22. R.N. Cooper, *Economic Policy in an Interdependent World* (Cambridge, Mass, 1966), pp. 108–12.

23. *The Collected Works of John Maynard Keynes,* Vol. XXV (Cambridge University Press, 1980), p. 31.

24. R.N. Cooper, *The Gold Standard: Historical Facts and Future Prospects* (Brookings Institution Paper 1, 1982), pp. 30–6, 48.

25. Robert Z. Aliber, *The International Money Game* (Basic Books), 1987, pp. 207–10.

26. Paul Davidson, *International Money and the Real World* (New York, John Wiley & Sons, 1982), pp. 155, 239.

CHAPTER FIVE

Role of the Voluntary Sector in Islam: A Conceptual Framework*

Introduction

This chapter discusses the role of the voluntary sector in the fulfilment of material and other needs within the family and in the provision of public goods. It focuses on the five traditional expressions of voluntary action on the part of the Muslim: family support, *zakāh* (wealth tax), gifts and grants, social service, and charitable endowments. The doctrine of *farḍ kifāyah* (socially-obligatory duties) is invoked to place voluntary action in its proper perspective. The chapter emphasizes the vast potential of the voluntary sector in contributing to the welfare of Muslim societies, especially in countries with Muslim minorities. Contemporary issues in the administration of *zakāh* and *waqf* (charitable endowments) are also examined in the light of *Sharī'ah*. Finally, some present trends and future possibilities in the development of the voluntary sector are noted with special reference to Islamic institutions.

Even though this volume is devoted to the state, a look at the voluntary sector is appropriate. The connecting link between the state and the voluntary sector at the conceptual level is *farḍ kifāyah*. The same social obligation which makes individuals establish the state is the well-spring of the voluntary sector in an Islamic society.

*The author gratefully acknowledges the comments made by Professors M. Anas Zarqa, Mohammed Ariff, and F.R. Faridi on an earlier draft of this chapter. Some insights provided by Professor Shamsher Ali at the workshop on 'Islam and the Economic Development of Southeast Asia: The Role of the Voluntary Sector', organized by the Institute of Southeast Asian Studies in Singapore, at which this chapter was presented as a paper, were very helpful in revising the work, for which I am grateful.

Islam's Emphasis on Voluntary Help

A Muslim individual should care for others – for their spiritual well-being, material welfare, individual needs and their collective or social good. Indeed, helping others is a basic rule of conduct in Islam. This is how a Muslim is characterized in the Qur'ān.

> And the believers, men and women, are protecting friends of one another; they enjoin the right and forbid the wrong . . . (9: 71).[1]

> Lo! those who believed and left their homes and strove with their wealth and their lives for the cause of Allah and those who took them in and helped them, these are protecting friends of one another . . . (8: 72).[2]

> Those who entered the city and the faith before them love those who flee unto them for refuge and find in their breasts no need for that which has been given them but prefer [the fugitives] above them though poverty become their lot. And whoso is saved from his own avarice – such are they who are successful (59: 9).[3]

> And [would assign] in all that they possessed a due share unto such as might ask [for help] and such as might suffer privation (51: 19).[4]

> So give the kinsman his due, and to the needy and to the wayfarer. That is for those who seek Allah's countenance. And such are successful (30: 38).[5]

> True piety does not consist in turning your faces towards the east or the west – but truly pious is he who believes in God, and the Last Day and the angels and revelation and the prophets; and spends his substance – however much he himself may cherish it – upon his near of kin, and the orphans, and the needy, and the wayfarer and the beggars and for the freeing of human beings from bondage, and is constant in prayers, and renders the purifying dues and [fully pious are] they who keep their promises whenever they promise and are patient in misfortune and hardship and in time of peril; it is they that have proved themselves true and it is they who are conscious of God (2: 177).[6]

Disregard for the plight of others is the hallmark of the unbelievers.

> And when it is said unto them: spend of that wherewith Allah has provided you, those who disbelieve say unto those who believe, shall we feed those whom Allah, if He willed, would feed? You are in naught else than error manifest (36: 47).[7]

> Have you observed him who believes in religion? That is he who repells the orphan, and urges not the feeding of the needy . . . (107: 1–3).[8]

Likewise the Prophet also emphasized the charitable nature of Muslims:

> 'Believers are to one another like a building whose parts support one another.' He then interlaced his fingers.[9]

> I am witness to the fact that all servants [of Allah] are brethren to one another.[10]

> Mankind are God's dependants so the most beloved of people in the sight of Allah are those who do good to His dependants.[11]

> Most liked by Allah is the man who is most beneficient to the people in general. And the most liked act is that of pleasing a Muslim or relieving him of some grief, or paying off a debt incurred by him, or saving him from hunger . . .[12]

> The Prophet once said, 'Charity is obligatory on every Muslim.' Asked if one has nothing to give in charity? He replied, 'He should work with his hands, then enjoy the fruits of his labour and give [something out of] it in charity.' Asked what if it is not possible for him to work, or if he does not work? He replied, 'He should help a needy person in distress.' Asked again what if even this he does not do? The Prophet replied, 'He should advise others to do good.' Asked what if he failed to do this also? The Prophet said, 'He should refrain from doing harm to others for even this is a charity from him.'[13]

It is clear in the light of the above verses from the Qur'ān and the traditions from the Prophet that the charitable behaviour required of a Muslim individual covers material support as well as spiritual and moral guidance, both by way of promoting goodness and preventing what is harmful. In fact, prevention of wrongdoing is especially declared to be a duty of every Muslim. The Prophet said:

> Whoever sees evil should strive to eradicate it. If he can do so by force, he should use force. If that is not possible he should speak out against it. If that is also not possible for him, he should at least abhor it in his heart, and that is the least that faith demands.[14]

Thus, the scope of voluntary action is not confined to the supply of economic goods and services. It encompasses non-material needs as well. Islam envisions a society in which individuals, while pursuing their self-interest, also care for the interests of others and everyone helps everyone else materially as well as morally so that all live a life that pleases Allah. The redistributive and allocative roles of the voluntary sector in an Islamic society can easily be gleaned through this vision which incorporates new concerns of social policy such as protection of the environment, supply of information, and social cohesion.

Voluntary Action

What is the source of voluntary action in man? What motivates him to be charitable? Though pushed to the sidelines by mainstream economics, a number of economists, starting with Adam Smith, have addressed this question, coming up with various answers.[15] It has been argued that voluntary action is born out of man's awareness of mutual interdependence. Self-interest itself urges one to help others in time of need. This explanation cannot, however, cover all observed voluntary action and is based on too narrow a concept of the 'economic man'. Non-selfish behaviour is an integral part of human behaviour. Altruism, defined as 'behaviour directed towards the benefit of others at some cost to the self where no extrinsic or *intrinsic* benefit is the primary intent of the behaviour',[16] is also part of human nature along with self-interest, especially after one has met his basic needs. More positive attitudes towards helping others and far-reaching voluntary action comes from love and from a sense of duty. Other motivating forces such as reputation and desire for recognition also play a significant role in eliciting voluntary action.

There is some truth in all these explanations, none of which need be interpreted so as to exclude the others. One must also add to the above list of motives, religious motivation, i.e. seeking the pleasure of Allah and reward in the Hereafter: one helps fellow human beings because one loves God and showing compassion to mankind is a channel through which to express one's love of God. It is not necessary for the purpose of our study to go into the details of this matter. It is necessary, however, to point out that social concern has been a fact of life in all human societies. It is only economic textbooks that ignore it! But the scope and strength of it varies from culture to culture. Religious cultures promote charitable behaviour and voluntary action while secular cultures undermine it, depending on the degree of emphasis on materialism and individualism. As we have seen above, Islam extols charitable behaviour, giving it a central place in its scheme of living. Moreover it gives it a universal orientation and secure foundation by rooting it in a Muslim's pursuit of the pleasure of Allah.

A voluntary act is one proceeding from one's own choice or consent. It follows that all action in pursuance of Islamic teachings is voluntary action. This also applies to what is obligatory in *Sharīʻah,* such as *zakāh,* as one's profession of faith is itself a voluntary action. Hence the voluntary activities of a Muslim include what is obligatory as well as what is recommended in Islam. The voluntary sector in an Islamic economy includes charitable activities, whether obligatory or recommended.

When an Islamic society is organized into a state where the *Sharīʻah* is sovereign, obligatory charities such as *zakāh* and *ʻushr*[17] are managed by the state. In a country where Muslims are in a minority, or in countries with a majority Muslim population where *Sharīʻah* is not implemented, there may be voluntary organizations managing these charities. Following the conceptual point made above, we will include all charitable activities in the voluntary sector, irrespective of the way they are organized and managed. This approach suits the contemporary reality in which the state's role in managing charities is minimal. It can also accommodate those periods of Islamic history in which the state played a more active role in this regard by keeping their management always separate from the administration of other state revenues,[18] in view of the religious nature of these charities.

Meeting Non-Material Needs

Despite some overlap due to expected reciprocity, the voluntary sector may be distinguished from the exchange economy where all action is based on some *quid pro quo* and where everything has a price. The exchange economy also has the distinctive feature of dealing only with measurables, because only measurable things can have a price expressible in terms of money, the medium of exchange. The voluntary sector is, sometimes, free of these constraints. There may not be *quid pro quo* involved directly and immediately. The objects of voluntary action may not be measurable. They need not have a price. Given these characteristics, the voluntary sector has an essential role in human society, as the many needs of man (psychological, aesthetic, and spiritual) depend on non-measurables for their fulfilment. Love and affection, approval and appreciation, recognition and praise, contentment and a sense of fulfilment, courtesies, etc., are some of the non-material non-measurables for which one cares so much in life, especially after one has met his biological needs. These needs are generally met by services, not by physical goods. These services, unlike the goods and services in the exchange economy, are not always characterized by scarcity. They do not necessarily involve any transfer of scarce resources. Their production is often costless, as is the case with the smile on one's face which cheers up someone else. The satisfaction of the psychological, aesthetic, and spiritual needs of people through acts of goodness is an important function of the voluntary sector, contributing in no small way to the sum total of human felicity.[19]

Even in the case of certain scarce goods, the voluntary sector performs better than the market. Human blood is a case in point.

A voluntary donor has no incentive to lie about his blood being free of disease.[20]

When the voluntary sector is dealing with goods and services which do carry a price because of scarcity (e.g. charitable giving of food) the transfer takes place more efficiently than in the exchange sector. The cost of such a transfer to the givers as well as to the society is only the cost of the resources forgone in the exchange sector. The givers do not seek a profit, hence their cost curves include neither monopoly rents nor the normal profits included in the cost curves in the exchange sector. The givers seek the pleasure of Allah, reward in the life after death, and/or love of their fellow human beings (which, in itself, derives from their love for Allah). The supply curve of resources to be transferred in charity is therefore a decreasing function of the cost of the transferred resources in the exchange sector but it is lower and flatter than it would have been if the transfer was effected in the exchange sector. The same supply curve is also an increasing function of the faith of the givers in the pleasure of Allah and reward in the Hereafter and love for fellow human beings. The stronger this faith the greater the supply at any given cost. This further depresses and flattens the supply curve. If the total amount of resources transferred on the basis of charity was to be effected through the exchange economy, two additional costs would have to be incurred. First, sufficient revenue would have to be mobilized through taxation, and this would involve the cost of administering the tax. Second, cash grants would have to be made to the recipients which would involve further administrative costs. It follows, therefore, that transfer of any amount of scarce resources to deserving recipients through charitable giving in the voluntary sector is more efficient than transfer of the same amount of resources through the market using the tax-subsidy mechanism. It may be noted that the social cost of transfer would increase further, if the government was obliged to resort to borrowing or to increasing the money supply in order to finance its welfare schemes.

The amount of resources actually transferred to the poor at any particular time may not, however, meet all the needs of the poor. A sound social redistributive policy is, therefore, called for so that the role of the voluntary sector is maximized, with the remaining gap being filled by fiscal measures. This is exactly what Islam seeks to do. According to this view, the role of charity is to correct the distortion effected by the working of a competitive system in the distribution of income and wealth, caused by disparities in the initial resource endowments as well as by malfunctioning of the competitive system. A further correction effected by public policies is needed, however, because of the failure of charity to eliminate poverty and undesirable disparities.

Need Fulfilment Within the Family

The family is the premier voluntary institution which is responsible, among other things, for the production and consumption of many goods and services outside the exchange economy. It is here that children are born, nursed, raised, and have their biological needs satisfied. While the family draws upon the exchange economy for the material goods and services it needs, services rendered by the mother, the father, and by other members are mixed with purchased goods and services in order to satisfy the various needs.

The fact that the services rendered by the family are largely missed by economic analysts should not deter us from realizing their crucial contribution to human welfare. Such a realization is necessary in order to appreciate the true nature and scope of the voluntary sector. The crucial point is: the family is not modelled on an exchange economy; it is a part of the voluntary sector. This view deepens our understanding of the family as well as of the voluntary sector.

Supply of Public Goods

The voluntary sector has an edge over both the private sector and the public sector in certain other areas, e.g. conflict resolution, information supply, and environmental protection. All three are in the nature of public goods which the market fails to provide or may not provide in the optimum way, on the basis of exchange alone. Public provision of these goods is costly and inefficient. The voluntary sector is better equipped, in these cases, to supply them by virtue of its altruistic forces and its capacity to mobilize time, energy, and skill free of cost or at minimal cost.

A major source of conflict in the free enterprise system has been the relations between organized labour and management. The exchange economy model, based on atomistic competition, has no internal mechanism for resolving this conflict. Introducing the state into this model does not help, as the forces operating in the model tend to make the state an instrument of one party to the conflict. It requires a non-selfish, non-partisan approach to ensure industrial peace. Beside basic reforms in the organization of industry, such as replacing fixed wages by sharing,[21] labour participation in management, and introduction of democratic methods of decision-making, voluntary arbitration and citizens' councils can play a significant role in this respect.

Economic decisions depend on information and the acquisition and processing of information absorb considerable resources. These costs increase with the size of the market.[22] The voluntary sector may not supplant the market, but it can reduce the costs of information if individuals and organizations are willing to volunteer information. Sometimes providing needed information does not involve any cost to the giver while it benefits the receiver. Voluntary organizations may gather and disseminate information relating to products, prices, job opportunities, markets, etc., to the benefit of consumers, labour, entrepreneurs, etc., at minimum cost.

What applies to information costs also applies to the cost of monitoring. When the implementation of an economic decision involves cooperation or compliance by others, there is a need to monitor its implementation. Monitoring has a cost. But the need to monitor, and hence the cost, will be less the more those involved are morally committed to the cause for which the decision is taken. Since voluntary action presupposes moral commitment, it can be concluded that voluntary implementation of a decision reduces the monitoring cost to society, as compared with that of the private sector.

Pollution threatens man's natural environment and the industrial civilization is destroying the ecological balance. Market failure inhibits the private sector to do the needful while the public sector is constrained by lack of information and resources. The voluntary sector may be more efficient in terms of both prevention and remedy. Preventive and remedial measures relating to pollution can be considered an Islamic duty. In the first instance, a conscious Muslim would desist from creating pollution, as he is required not to harm others. Secondly, people in the neighbourhood would protest against policies which are destructive of the environment. Thirdly, when some remedial measures are to be taken, a sense of Islamic duty would counteract the selfish motive to 'free ride'. In fact, Islamic motivation would mobilize voluntary services for the preservation of a healthy environment. Islamic values persuade economic agents to sacrifice private advantage for the sake of public interest. The voluntary sector may, therefore, effectively supplement the public sector in protecting the environment.

This line of reasoning can also be extended to other public and quasi-public goods such as education, health, scientific research, etc. The voluntary sector is already playing an important role in these areas in advanced countries like the United States. In fact, these are some of the areas in which the voluntary sector has been very active in Muslim societies as well, as the brief historical survey below will show. The supply of public and quasi-public goods by the voluntary sector relieves the public sector of some responsibilities which it would otherwise have to shoulder, thereby preventing the public sector from becoming too large.

Redistributive and Allocative Role of the Voluntary Sector

The voluntary sector can play a major redistributive role by effecting a transfer of resources from the rich to the poor more efficiently than the state, as the costs of the transfer may be less and identification of the needy (especially among relatives, in neighbourhoods, and at local levels) may be more accurate. As the following description of the traditional categories of voluntary action in an Islamic society demonstrates, a substantial redistribution is in fact envisaged through the voluntary sector in an Islamic society.

The recipients' marginal propensity to consume being

presumably higher than those of the givers, the preferences of the (poor) recipients are also likely to differ from those of the (rich) givers. Most of the resources transferred voluntarily to the poor may be used for the fulfilment of basic needs, such as food, shelter, education, health, etc. The net impact of the transfer may, therefore, be an increase in the demand for essential goods and services. This implies a significant allocative role for the voluntary sector.

Sometimes the voluntary sector itself produces goods and services allocated directly to the needy. Consider, for example, the case of the person teaching, in his spare time, free of charge, the illiterate in the neighbourhood to read and write.

Traditional Expressions of Voluntary Action

Thus far, we have focused on the role of the voluntary sector in a wide sense. We shall now proceed to examine voluntary economic activities in an Islamic society in terms of certain familiar categories. This should not be taken to imply that the voluntary sector in an Islamic society is confined to certain traditional activities. On the contrary, these categories provide the means and a framework for a wider role of the voluntary sector in a modern Islamic society.

For the sake of convenience, voluntary activities in an Islamic society can be studied under the following five categories:

1. Obligatory family support.
2. *Zakāh, 'ushr,* and *ṣadaqat al-fiṭr (fiṭrah).*
3. Gifts and grants in cash, kind or usufruct.
4. Voluntary social service.
5. Charitable endowments *(waqf).*

A brief description of each is in order.

Obligatory Family Support. The basic institution in an Islamic society is the family. The economics of the family is built around the husband's obligation to support his wife financially irrespective of her financial condition. He is also obliged to support his minor children. The jurists are also unanimously of the view that every person is obliged to support his parents and his adult offspring, including the unmarried, divorced, or widowed daughter, in case they have no means to support themselves, provided he has the means to do so. This obligation extends to some other blood relations too, but the jurists differ on the details. The predominant view, however, is that the financial support of an indigent person devolves on those who would inherit from him if he dies leaving some property, and that this responsibility is to be shared in the same proportions in which that inheritance would be shared.[23] To complete the picture, it may also be noted that, according to *Sharī'ah,* the financial support of a person who has no one to support him devolves on the Islamic state.[24] Thus, the doctrine of obligatory maintenance allowances (*al-nafaqāt al-wājibah*) provides for every indigent person in an Islamic society.

The first line of defence in the Islamic scheme of providing for the needy is the family. As we shall see below, *zakāh, ṣadaqah* (voluntary charity), etc., buttress the defences further so that no human being goes without fulfilment of basic needs. As it stands, the above rule is designed to serve the purpose regardless of whether one is living in an Islamic state or is the citizen of a Muslim-minority country. It is interesting to note that the above rule relating to obligatory family support was recently invoked in the controversy arising from the famous Shah Bano case in India, resulting in its incorporation in the Muslim Personal Laws as enforced in the country.[25] It is significant to note that the role assigned to the Islamic state, as the source of support for an indigent person in the last resort, has been assigned by that legislation to the institution of *awqāf* (charitable endowments), in so far as the support of a divorced woman is concerned.[26]

In accordance with the conceptual point noted above, namely that fulfilment of religious obligations is to be considered as voluntary action, the system of obligatory maintenance allowances outlined above is an integral part of the voluntary sector in an Islamic society, notwithstanding any legal backing provided to it. Emphasis on this system and proper education of the community on this point can go a long way in increasing solidarity and cohesion in the institution of the family which would otherwise be threatened by the pervasive individualism and materialism of modern secular culture. The shrinkage of the family to the nuclear family in modern secular societies and its frequent break-up due to divorce have been partly responsible for transferring the social security system to the state. A large part of this system was traditionally taken care of by the extended family, at a much lower cost to society than that which state systems entail.

Zakāh and *'Ushr*. *Zakāh* concretizes the obligation towards others as analyzed at the outset. It gives the right orientation to a Muslim's behaviour.

Every Muslim with some means – specified in the relevant rules – has to give away a certain portion of his possessions to those mentioned in the Qur'ānic verse:

> The alms are for the poor and the needy, and those who collect them, and those whose hearts are to be reconciled, and to free the captives and the debtors, and for the cause of Allah, and [for] the wayfarer; a duty imposed by Allah. Allah is Knower, Wise (9: 60).[27]

The coverage of *zakāh* is very wide. It can be summarized as follows:

1. Capital assets: grazing animals and stock in trade, i.e., all that is meant to be traded, including machinery, property, and shares and common stock.
2. Savings in cash, gold, and silver.
3. Current income in the form of agricultural produce, minerals, and marine products.

Provided one's holdings are above a specified threshold (*niṣāb*), which is different for the different categories mentioned above, one's entire holdings (and not only what is above *niṣāb*) are liable to *zakāh*. The rates applicable to animals are detailed in the relevant sources. The *zakāh* rate for cash, gold and silver holdings, and stock in trade is 2.5 per cent. The rate applicable to agricultural produce is 10 per cent or 5 per cent, depending on whether it is irrigated by rain or by man-made means. Scholars differ as to the rate for minerals and marine products.[28] Opinions also differ regarding the *zakāh* rate on honey and other wealth acquired from forests.[29]

Zakāh is to be assessed annually except in the case of agricultural produce, mineral wealth, and marine products, which is to be paid as and when they accrue.

As the Qur'ānic verse quoted above lays down, *zakāh* is meant mainly for the poor. Some *zakāh* can be spent, however, for meeting the cost of *zakāh* administration. But the expenditure of *zakāh* revenue 'in the cause of Allah' and 'for those whose hearts are to be reconciled' to Islam stands on a different footing. Here it is the defence and promotion of Islam that is in question. No strict rules are laid down for the distribution of *zakāh* revenue over the specified heads of expenditure, leaving some room for discretion. But the first charge on *zakāh* revenue from any unit of population – village, town, or region – is the needs of that unit. *Zakāh* collected from a region may be transferred to another region only after meeting the needs of that region.[30] This rule implies that *'ushr* revenue from the rural areas should preferably be devoted to removal of rural poverty. *Zakāh* may be disbursed in cash or kind. There is no prescribed limit for what a single person or family may receive out of *zakāh* during a year, but most of the scholars who raised this question agree that the entire annual expenses of a recipient may be met out of *zakāh* funds,[31] if funds are available.

As the Qur'ānic verse 9: 103 provides, it is the prerogative of an Islamic state to collect *zakāh* and *'ushr*. *Zakāh* was, in fact, collected and disbursed by the state in early Islamic history. However, from the time of Caliph 'Uthmān onwards assessment and payment of *zakāh* on non-apparent wealth, i.e., cash, gold, and silver, was left to individuals. But a Muslim's duty to pay *zakāh* does not devolve on the existence of an Islamic state or the summons of a *zakāh* collector. Like daily prayers and fasting in the month of Ramaḍān, it is a Muslim's duty to assess and give away the *zakāh* due on his possessions. Throughout Islamic history, conscientious Muslims have been fulfilling this obligation on their own as well as through religious and social organizations, when the state was not administering *zakāh*. Besides providing much needed help to the poor and supporting essential Islamic activities, this practice has been instrumental in maintaining solidarity in the community, especially in countries with Muslim minorities.

Zakāh is collected and distributed by the state only in some

Muslim countries.[32] In many other Muslim countries and countries with Muslim minorities there are numerous national, regional, or local organizations administering *zakāh* on a voluntary basis. But a sizeable part of *zakāh* is distributed by the *zakāh* payers directly to the poor in the locality. As a result of these decentralized and *ad hoc* arrangements, there is no uniform policy on a number of issues relating to *zakāh* administration which arise in the modern context. Some of these are noted below:

1. Should the *zakāh* funds lie idle while awaiting disbursement or can they be invested with a view to increasing the benefit eventually accruing to the recipients?
2. Must *zakāh* be transferred to its beneficiaries in cash or kind (in case it is collected in kind), or can it be given in the form of tools of trade, agricultural equipment, etc., to help the working poor on a more durable basis?
3. Can *zakāh* funds be used for establishing and financing institutions that generate services, e.g., education, training, medical care, with the provision that only the poor get these services free of cost?
4. Can *zakāh* funds be used to give productive loans to the poor?
5. Can *zakāh* funds be used for the defence and promotion of Islam in the form of free distribution of Islamic literature, employing paid preachers, organizing conferences, etc.?
6. Can *zakāh* funds be used for building mosques and religious schools in Muslim-minority countries?

Most traditional scholars would not answer these questions in the affirmative. But some contemporary scholars have convincingly argued in favour of some of these policies.[33]

A policy of helping the able-bodied poor out of poverty and enabling them to earn their living is definitely desirable and *zakāh* funds can play at least a partial role in this respect, even while avoiding the expenditure policies which fail to gain a consensus of the *Sharī'ah* scholars. The remaining part of the expenditure can be met out of voluntary charitable donations and general revenue of the state.

It is also important, especially in the case of countries with

Muslim minorities, to adopt a model of *zakāh* administration which responds to the diversity in local needs. A chain of local committees knit together under regional councils and ultimately guided by a representative body at the national level seems to be an appropriate model. One can draw upon the Pakistani experience[34] as well as suggestions made by some economists.[35]

Some recently established Islamic financial institutions are also collecting and distributing *zakāh* (from the public in general and not only from their shareholders and depositors). In the absence of any proper evaluation of this very recent practice, which is confined to a few places, it is difficult to comment on the appropriateness of this arrangement. On the one hand, these modern institutions are better equipped to handle the accounts and follow the guide-lines laid down for them as compared to the numerous voluntary organizations that are presently doing the job. On the other hand, the job does not fit in with the main profit-making activities of these institutions. Some empirical studies are needed for a proper examination of this issue.

What is beyond controversy, however, is the need for a handy *zakāh* manual to guide individual as well as institutional *zakāh* payers in assessing their *zakāh* liabilities and identifying optimal ways of allocating *zakāh* funds.

Ṣadaqah al-Fiṭr. This refers to charity given on conclusion of the month-long fasting in Ramaḍān to ensure that no one suffers privation during the annual *'Īd* celebrations which immediately follow the last day of Ramaḍān. Every Muslim of some means should pay, for himself as well as on behalf of his dependents. The *fiṭr* payment thus amounts to a poll tax. It is specified in terms of some staple food, e.g. wheat, barley, dates, the quantity to be given away being a little above 2 kg.[36] It should be handed over directly to the deserving poor as far as possible. Neither a postponement of payment to some future date nor a transfer to some other locality is desirable. Three out of the four main schools of Islamic law insist on the payment of this charity in kind, but the Ḥanafī school allows payment in cash and a number of contemporary scholars regard cash payments as being more convenient for both the givers and the recipients.[37]

Unlike *zakāh, ṣadaqah al-fiṭr* was not collected and distributed by the early Islamic states. Person-to-person transfers were easily possible in view of the comparatively smaller population living in a town or village. The multi-million metropolis of contemporary societies may sometimes defy this solution. The practice of voluntary organizations taking up the task of collecting and distributing this charity is now fairly widespread, without inviting disapproval from scholars.

The obligatory charities discussed above have enormous potentialities for mobilizing a sizeable fund dedicated mainly to the eradication of poverty. It has been estimated that the annual yield of *zakāh* in a Muslim country would be around 3 per cent of the gross domestic product.[38] The corresponding collection from Muslims living in countries with Muslim minorities would also be substantial. Even though the charity on the eve of *'Īd* is a modest amount, more people are obliged to pay it, for themselves and on behalf of their dependents, than those who are liable to pay *zakāh*. Given proper management, these charities can go a long way in alleviating suffering and eliminating privation.

Recommended Charities. Recommended charities are designed to fill any gap that obligatory charities may leave, in order to complete the task of need fulfilment. They may also take care of social needs not covered by *zakāh* expenditures. No rates have been prescribed for non-obligatory charities. Nevertheless, there is a general consideration of vital importance which sets a *required* minimum at the social level: enough charities should be available to ensure the fulfilment of basic individual needs and essential social needs. This is the essence of the doctrine of *farḍ kifāyah*, or socially-obligatory duties. We have already discussed them in Chapters One and Two above. But a brief recapitulation seems to be in order.

Socially-obligatory duties are those which the Law-Giver wants carried out, irrespective of who does them. They must be performed so that the needful is done, lest all those who are capable of performing them become sinful. In other words, these duties are directed at ensuring the common interests of a community of individuals, not devolving on particular individuals, so that if some perform them and the relevant purpose is served, others will be absolved of the responsibility.

No closed list of socially-obligatory duties is handed down by *Sharī'ah* even though a number of them have found specific mention. Any activity that is necessary for safeguarding the vital interests of the people relating to survival and Islamic living is to be considered a socially-obligatory duty. Those specifically mentioned include need fulfilment, *da'wah* (communicating the message of Allah to mankind), enjoining right conduct and forbidding wrong (*al-amr bi'l-mar'ūf wa'l-nahy 'an al-munkar*), and physical and ideological defence of the community of Islam. Even the institution of a ruler to govern the community in accordance with *Sharī'ah* (i.e. establishment of an Islamic state) is a *farḍ kifāyah*.[39] For Muslims living under Islamic rule, the state becomes the discharger of socially-obligatory duties, in the last resort. In the absence of such a state, alternative arrangements are necessary to protect the vital interests of the community. The nature of the voluntary sector in a Muslim society that is deprived of Islamic rule has to be studied in this perspective. This is especially important in the case of countries with Muslim minorities where Islamic rule is not feasible. It is only the voluntary sector that can protect these interests. In other words, the Islamic voluntary sector in a society with a minority of Muslims has to discharge many religious and welfare functions which are, in normal circumstances, discharged by the Islamic state.

It is the community's awareness of this crucial fact that has led to the emergence, throughout Islamic history, of revivalist movements, institutions for religious education, and community courts for settling disputes according to *Sharī'ah* (in particular, disputes relating to marriage, divorce, guardianship, etc.).

What is the significance of regarding all these activities as socially-obligatory duties? Two points may be noted. Firstly, the sense of a religious duty ensures that the relevant activity will take place even though neither self-interest nor the coercive power of the state is there to ensure it. This point is of special importance for the Muslim minorities. Secondly, the nature of *farḍ kifāyah* requires vigilance on the part of every individual who is capable of performing it. Even when such an individual is in no position to perform a socially-obligatory duty, he must observe whether the needful is being done by some other individuals so that he is, ultimately, absolved of *his* religious obligations.

The care for social interest as distinguished from self-interest is the most significant dimension to the doctrine of *farḍ kifāyah*. Vigilance on the part of every individual possessing the ability to perform a particular duty, and the awareness of its being a *religious* duty, raises the chances of that duty being performed.

Gifts and Grants. Unilateral transfers in cash or kind have been the main expression of charitable behaviour throughout history. Such acts of charity may benefit a relative, a friend, a neighbour, a needy person who asks for it, or a needy person to whom the giver himself reaches out. Charity may go to a social institution like an orphanage, a school, a hospital, a rest-room for the wayfarer, or to an organization propagating religion. It may sometimes go to the state in response to an appeal for funds in an emergency caused by war, famine, flood, epidemic, etc. Greatly encouraged by Islam, charitable giving has been widely practised in Muslim societies.

Since Islam prohibits charging interest on loans, lending is also a charitable act. The Prophet said, 'Every loan is a charity.'[40] So is lending durable articles, of use, e.g. utensils, vehicles, equipment. Refusal to do so is mentioned in the Qur'ān as characteristic of the unbelievers (107: 7). The Prophet also recommended exchange of gifts as it contributes to mutual love and affection. He said:

> Shake hands, it will remove rancour, and make gifts to one another [as a result] you will love each other and it will remove malice.[41]

One can also give away a part of one's legacy in charity. The Islamic laws of inheritance call for a fair distribution among his nearest relatives of what a deceased person has left. Under Islamic laws, one's will cannot modify this distribution as a will cannot be made in favour of an heir. The permission to will away up to a third of the legacy is designed to provide for charities as well as for distant relatives not covered by the law in a particular case. This provision has been widely utilized for making bequests for charitable purposes. Every Muslim is expected to take due notice of the Prophet's remark that:

> When a man dies his [good] deeds stop, except through three [channels]: A charity which continues [giving its benefits] or knowledge that can be utilized or an offspring with good conduct who prays for him.[42]

Social Service. Services rendered free of charge to meet individual needs or promote social welfare are also an important form of charity. Participating in a literary drive, planting trees, building a dam, and volunteering to defend the community against external aggression are some of the myriad forms such charity might take. Devoting one's spare time to social service adds to the sum total of human welfare at little or no cost to society. Islam has urged its followers to volunteer for these services. At the same time it wants them to distribute their energies wisely between various kinds of social needs, e.g. between defence and (religious) education.

> . . . it is not desirable that all of the believers take the field [in time of war]. From within every group in their midst, some shall refrain from going forth to war, and shall devote themselves [instead] to acquiring deep knowledge of the Faith, and [thus be able to] teach their home coming brethren, so that these [too] might guard themselves against evil (9: 122).[43]

Endowments. The emphasis Islam places on contributing to the good of society has prompted wealthy Muslims to go beyond *ad hoc* charity to making permanent provisions for supporting welfare activities. Some of them have made special arrangements whereby property is dedicated to a cause so that only the income flowing from it is available for current expenditure in that cause. This is referred to as *waqf* (endowments).

> It is reported that the son of 'Umar said, 'Some land in Khaybar fell to the lot of 'Umar.' He came to the Prophet, and said, 'I got a land such as I never had a property better than it, so what do you advise me regarding it?' The Prophet said, 'If you wish you can give it away in charity detaining its corpus.' So 'Umar gave it away in charity providing that its corpus may neither be sold nor gifted nor

could it be inherited. It would be meant for the poor, the relatives, for freeing slaves, for the cause of Allah, for guests and for the wayfarer. It would be permissible for its custodian to eat out of it according to convention or feed a friend, without making it a source of personal wealth.[44]

The Voluntary Sector in Islamic History

The various forms of charitable giving, seen in the broad perspective of socially-obligatory duties (*farḍ kifāyah*), provide a very wide scope for the voluntary sector in an Islamic society. They reinforce the vision that an Islamic society is a cooperative affair in which every individual, once he has ensured the fulfilment of his own needs through his own labour and inherited wealth, if any, volunteers to take care of the needs of other fellow humans and of the social and collective needs according to his capacity. This is evidenced in Islamic history, especially in its early golden period. It will, therefore, be instructive to look at the voluntary sector throughout Islamic history before we proceed to examine its contemporary status.

Both voluntary services and voluntary charity in cash or kind played a big role in Madīnah during the time of the Prophet. The Madīnah mosque, named after the Prophet, was constructed by voluntary labour. Muslim residents of Madīnah accommodated the migrants from Makkah (the *muhājirīn*) and hosted them, even shared their properties with them, till they were able to find work and establish themselves.[45] Some of the earliest endowments in Islamic society were created in this period.[46] The numerous battles to ward off the attacking Makkans were all fought by volunteer forces. Thus, the entire fabric of the early Islamic society was built around voluntary services and charitable givings, till the public treasury (*Bayt al-Māl*) was established with permanent sources of income like *zakāh, 'ushr,* and *kharāj* (land tax). The situation during the next thirty years of pious rule of the four great Caliphs remained more or less the same although the relative prosperity during the latter half of this period might have reduced the need for private charity. Nevertheless, charitable endowments continued to be created.[47]

The role of the voluntary sector in the later period of Islamic history has to be studied largely in terms of charitable endowments as no data are available for the other forms of voluntary activities, such as family support, *zakāh,* grants, and social services. It can be safely assumed, however, that a society which produced a wide network of charitable endowments covering almost all social services and welfare activities must have responded warmly to individual needs for succour.

There are four aspects of *waqf* throughout Islamic history which call for attention: their purpose, the kinds of properties involved, their management, and the kind of supervision exercised by the courts or the government.

As regards the purposes for which charitable endowments were made (as distinguished from family endowments[48] which do not concern us in this study), almost all kinds of social services were involved. These included, to name a few, education at all levels, facilities for prayers and other religious rites, health facilities ranging from hospitals to homes for the disabled, parks, inns and rest-rooms, drinking water facilities, food distribution centres, and animal care centres.

As regards the types of properties involved, almost every kind of property capable of yielding an income or giving some benefits was endowed. Agricultural land, residential buildings, schools, wells, baths, bakeries, godowns, etc., in various parts of the land were all dedicated by their owners to the needy. Islamic law also provides for endowing a sum of money, to be put in trust, so that its profits are given away as charity.[49]

The management of *waqf* properties was vested in a supervisor nominated by the donor and the *waqf* deed also stipulated who would succeed the supervisor.

In the early period, the state did not have a clearly defined role *vis-à-vis* the *waqf* properties and their management, but the courts did look into any complaints relating to their mismanagement. In the later period, we find increasing state involvement in *waqf* management owing to a number of causes, the chief one being widespread abuse of powers by *waqf* supervisors. Another reason for increased state intervention was the fact that *waqf* properties were exempt from taxes. This resulted in substantial loss of revenue to the state as more and more properties, especially agricultural land, were converted into *waqf*. This forced the state to take over some *waqf* properties, especially in times of financial crisis caused by wars.[50]

The Ottomans formed a Ministry of Waqf in 1840, establishing a tradition that continues in almost every Muslim country, as well as in some countries with Muslim minorities, such as India and the Philippines, in modern times.

Some Special Features of *Waqf*

Waqf properties have some special features distinguishing them from private and public properties. While these features confer some benefits on society which cannot be derived from private or public properties, they also pose some problems.

Waqf takes a property out of individual ownership, vesting the ownership in Allah. A *waqf* property is not a state property just as it is not a private property. *Waqf* is permanent and irrevocable, hence the act of endowment is irreversible. With the passage of time, private properties pass into the *waqf* sector but the reverse does not and cannot take place.

Since *waqf* is made by the rich and the society in general and the poor in particular benefit from the endowment, the above features serve to mitigate the ill effects of inequality in the distribution of income and wealth. Unlike the short-term impact of government budgetary policies, the institution of *waqf* over time counteracts the tendency towards concentration of wealth.

But problems arise as more and more properties, especially agricultural land and urban properties, are turned into *waqf*. The urge to maximize the returns – the engine of growth in the private sector – has not been a prominent feature of *waqf* management. The *waqf* sector operates largely outside the competitive market, resulting in sluggishness and stagnation. As *waqf* properties are exempt from taxes, a growing *waqf* sector would reduce the fiscal resources of the state.

Another feature of *waqf* is the supremacy of the will of the *wāqif* (the *waqf* maker) with respect to its purpose, beneficiaries, and management. In addition to the macro-economic problem noted above, this feature poses a number of problems at the micro-economic level.

Historically, tough problems were posed by the family *waqf*, which we do not propose to discuss in this chapter as it has been abolished in most places.[51] Moreover, it does not fall fully in the voluntary sector category as noted above. But, even in the case of charitable endowments, problems arise because sometimes the *wāqif* defines the purposes very specifically and narrowly. As circumstances change, with the passage of time, some of these purposes may become redundant or even anti-social. In such a situation there is a need to subject the will of the *wāqif* to the supremacy of public purpose (*maṣlaḥah 'āmmah*) and objectives of *Sharī'ah* (*maqāṣid al-sharī'ah*). It will be recalled that even the exercise of individual ownership rights is subject to these overriding considerations. There is no reason why properties dedicated to social welfare should not be subject to the same considerations.

A *waqf* is normally managed by a custodian (*mutawallī*) named by the *wāqif*. The *waqf* deed also provides for a successor to the custodian in the event of his death or incapacity, and how to deal with mismanagement. These provisions may not, however, be satisfactory or comprehensive enough, thereby inviting intervention by the courts or the state. The circumstances justifying intervention, as well as the scope of such intervention, have been discussed in the *fiqh* (jurisprudence) literature and enshrined in the *waqf* laws of various countries. Actual experience and new exigencies continue to necessitate fresh enactments. But there is an ever-present danger of appropriation of *waqf* properties by the state under one excuse or another. This has happened throughout history in Muslim countries and countries with Muslim minorities. Such state take-overs on a large scale have dampened the people's enthusiasm to create charitable endowments.

Thus the voluntary sector, especially *waqf*, has to be guarded against misappropriation by the state as well as mismanagement by individuals or organizations which manage the endowments. Only vigilance on the part of the people in general can ensure this. As regards mismanagement of endowments, corrective action may come from three directions; the public (especially the beneficiaries), the courts, and the state acting through its legislative and executive branches to streamline the laws and regulations governing *waqf* properties and implementing them meticulously.

In contemporary circumstances, a more serious threat comes from the tendency to incorporate *waqf* in the public sector, especially in countries with Muslim minorities. This threat can be countered only if the people have a clear perception of the need for, and distinctive role of, the *waqf* sector, justifying its separate existence. As noted above the Prophet, when asked by 'Umar, did not advise him to give away his property (in this case a fertile land) to the state, even though he himself was the head of state. Instead, he advised 'Umar to make a *waqf*. This advice implies that the Prophet visualized a useful role for *waqf* alongside the public sector.

Future Prospects

We have already noted the trend towards an increasing role of the state in the management of *waqf*. What about the role of *waqf* itself? It is not far-fetched to surmise that the role of *waqf* is likely to increase in countries with Muslim minorities but not in countries where the majority of the population is Muslim. The reason for a more active role for *waqf* in the former lies in the increasing Islamic awareness in these communities coupled with the realization that, with a state which is at best indifferent to their religion and to many of their special socio-economic needs, they have to use *waqf* for the fulfilment of these needs and for the protection and promotion of Islam. For historical reasons, the legitimacy of *waqf* and its role in the religious and social life of the community is well established and accepted by the (ruling) majority. On the other hand, increasing Islamic awareness makes Muslims in countries where they form a majority press their rulers to adopt more Islamic policies. There is no pressure on *waqf* as such, unless rulers respond to popular pressure by activating the *waqf*.

Apart from *waqf*, however, there is a greater recourse everywhere to voluntary action for the promotion of Islam and the improvement of socio-economic conditions of the community. Government failure (due to a lack of will as well as the sluggishness of the bureaucracy) and market failure (due to lack of motivation) draw more energies towards the voluntary sector to do the needful for the betterment of the *ummah*. We can, therefore, expect some improvement in *waqf* management and a greater mobilization of charities, regular as well as *ad hoc*. One can reasonably expect better facilities for offering prayers, increased publication and distribution of Islamic literature, and more educational institutions that include Islamic courses in the curricula. This would be more true of the Muslim communities living as minorities where one also notices a greater mobilization for the protection of Muslim personal laws, crucial for the cultural identity of the communities.

The emergence of Islamic financial institutions that operate without interest is an important development in the voluntary sector. It is a product of the community's desire to avoid interest while ensuring full participation in the modern exchange economy. Once such an institution is established it may also cater to some other socio-economic needs of the community, such as investment of (temporary) surpluses in charitable funds, (interest-free) loans to social and educational institutions, even collection and disbursement of charity. Its greater role lies in mobilizing savings by providing Islamically permissible avenues of investment and supplying needed capital to small businessmen in the community. A modest beginning of the Islamic financial movement goes back half a century, but it came to the forefront in the 1970s. Despite some stagnation, it has now reached many countries, including those in which Muslims are a minority, and includes banking institutions, investment companies, credit unions, and insurance companies.[52]

We conclude this study on an optimistic note regarding the role of the voluntary sector in contemporary Muslim societies. It is venturing into some new areas and, at the same time, showing greater vigour in traditional spheres. In view of the conceptual framework presented in this chapter, one cannot miss the direct relationship between this renewed vigour of the voluntary sector and ongoing Islamic resurgence. Thanks to this resurgence, one can look forward to increasing 'Islamization' of the economies in countries where Muslims are a majority and an enlargement of the Islamic voluntary sector in countries where Muslims are a minority.

Notes

1. M.M. Pickthall, *The Meaning of the Glorious Qur'ān* (Makkah, The Muslim World League, 1977). In the parentheses following the Qur'ānic verses the first number indicates the *Sūrah* (Chapter) while the second indicates the verse.

2. *Ibid.*

3. *Ibid.*

4. Muhammad Asad, *The Meaning of the Qur'ān* (London, 1980).

5. Pickthall, *op. cit.*

6. Asad, *op. cit.*

7. Pickthall, *op. cit.*

8. *Ibid.*

9. Muḥammad bin Ismā'īl al-Bukhārī, *Kitāb al-Ṣalāt, Bāb Tashbīk al-Aṣābi' fī'l-Masjid wa Ghayrih.*

10. Abū Dāwūd, *Kitāb al-Ṣalāt, Bāb mā yaqūl al-Rajul idhā sallam.*

11. Al-Khaṭīb al-'Umarī, *Bāb al-Shafaqah wa'l-Raḥmah 'alā'l-Khalq.*

12. Al-Ṭabarānī, *al-Mu'jam al-Ṣaghīr* (Delhi, Maṭba'at al-Anṣar, 1311 AH), p. 179.

13. Al-Bukhārī, *Kitāb al-Ādāb, Bāb Kullu ma'rūf Ṣadaqah.*

14. Abū Dāwūd, *Kitāb al-Ṣalāt, Bāb Khuṭbat Yawm al-'Īd.*

15. For a brief history see David Collard, *Altruism and Economy: A Study in Non-Selfish Behaviour* (Oxford, Martin Robertson, 1978), pp. 51–64 and Mark A. Lutz and Kenneth Lux, *The Challenge of Humanistic Economics* (Menlo Park, California, Benjamin/Cummings Publishing Company, 1979), pp. 28–58. Some answers to the above question may be found in these two sources, and also in *Altruism and Helping Behaviour: Personality and Development Perspective*, ed. J. Philippe Rushton and Richard M. Sorrentino (Hellsdale, New Jersey, Lawrence Elbaum Associates, 1981).

16. Rushton and Sorrentino (*op. cit.*, p. 427). For an alternative definition, see Bela Balassa and Richard Nelson (eds.), *Economic Progress, Private Values and Public Policy: Essays in Honour of William Fellner* (Amsterdam, 1977), p. 181.

17. *'Ushr* is a variant of *Zakāh*: one-tenth of the produce of rain-irrigated land payable to the state.

18. This lends further credence to our inclusion of religious obligations like *zakāh* in the voluntary sector. As pointed out above, this inclusion is justified by the present reality in which obligatory charities are, generally speaking, not enforced by the state. Moreover, the classification adopted by us suits this study which focuses on the role of the voluntary sector as distinguished from the public sector and the private sector.

19. Hence the precious piece of Prophetic wisdom: 'Do not regard as a petty thing any act of goodness, even meeting your brother with a cheerful face.' Narrated by Abū Dharr in Muslim, *Kitāb al-Birr wa'l-Ṣadaqah, Bāb istiḥbāb Ṭalāqat al-wajh 'inda'l-Liqā'*.

20. Peker Singer, 'Freedom and Utilities in the Distribution of Health Care' in *Market and Morals,* ed. Gerald Dovorkin, Gordon Bermant, and Peter G. Brown (Washington, Hampshire Publishing Company, 1977), p. 165.

21. Martin L. Weitzman, *The Share Economy* (Cambridge, Mass., Harvard University Press, 1984).

22. Peter G. Elkan, *The New Model Economy* (New York, Pergamon Press, 1982), p. 65.

23. Aḥmad Ibrāhīm Ibrāhīm, *Niẓām al-Nafaqāt fi'l-Sharī'ah al-Islāmīyah* (1394 AH). 'Abd al-Raḥmān al-Jazīrī, *Kitāb al-Fiqh 'alā al-Madhāhib al-Arba'ah.* Vol. 3, *Mabāḥith al-Nafaqāt* (Cairo, Sharkit Fann al-Ṭibā'ah).

24. See Chapter One, points 3 to 9.

25. The Muslim Women (Protection of Rights on Divorce) Act, 1986. For its text see *Muslim India* (Delhi), Vol. IV, No. 40 (April 1986), pp. 154–5.

26. *Muslim India, ibid.*

27. Pickthall, *op. cit.*

28. Yūsuf al-Qaraḍāwī, *Fiqh al-Zakāt* (Beirut, 1981), pp. 432–56.

29. *Ibid.*, pp. 425–31; M. Raquibuzzaman, *Some Administrative Aspect of Collection and Disbursement of Zakat* (Jeddah, Centre for Research in Islamic Economics, 1987).

30. Al-Qaraḍāwī, *op. cit.*, pp. 809–20.

31. *Ibid.*, pp. 563–74.

32. See Rafīq al-Miṣrī's translation (with an introduction) of *The Zakat Manual* issued by the Central Zakat Administration of Pakistan, *Kitāb al-Zakāh* (Jeddah, Centre for Research in Islamic Economics, 1984), pp. 9–83, for a review of the *zakāh* laws in Pakistan, Sudan, Saudi Arabia, and Libya. Malaysia and Bangladesh also have state agencies for the collection and disbursement of *zakāh*.

33. See, for example, the relevant sections of al-Qaraḍāwī (*op. cit.*); Sayyid Abū'l A'lā al-Mawdūdī, *Fatāwā al-Zakāh,* trans. Rafīq al-Miṣrī (Jeddah, Centre for Research in Islamic Economics, 1985); Raquibuzzaman (*op. cit.*); and Muḥammad 'Abd al-Qādir Abū Fāris, *Infāq fi'l-Maṣāliḥ al-'Āmmah* ('Ammān, Dār al-Furqān, 1983).

34. Central Zakat Administration, *The Zakat Manual* (Islamabad: Ministry of Finance, Government of Pakistan, 1982).

35. Raquibuzzaman, *op. cit.*

36. According to the Ḥanafī school the quantity of wheat to be given away is only half of this, i.e. a little above 1 kg., while in the case of barley, etc., it is a little above 2 kg.

37. Al-Qaraḍāwī, *op. cit.*, pp. 948–9.

38. Muhammad Anas Zarqa, 'Islamic Distributive Schemes' in *Distributive Justice and Need Fulfilment in an Islamic Economy,* ed. Munawar Iqbal (Islamabad, International Institute of Islamic Economics, 1986), p. 178.

39. Al-Māwardī, *al-Aḥkām al-Sulṭānīyah* (1978), p. 5.

40. Al-Ṭabarānī, *op. cit.*, p. 80.

41. Mālik bin Anas, *al-Muwaṭṭa'; Kitāb Ḥusn al-Khuluq, Bāb Mā Jā'a fī'l-Muhājarah.*

42. Muḥammad bin Ismā'īl al-Bukhārī, *al-Adab al-Mufrad, Bāb birr al-wālidayn* (Beirut, Dar Maktabat al-Ḥayāt, 1980), p. 15.

43. Asad, *op. cit.*

44. Muḥammad bin Ismā'īl al-Bukhārī, *al-Jāmi' al-Ṣaḥīḥ, Kitāb al-Waṣāyā.*

45. Aḥmad bin Yaḥyā bin Jābir al-Balādhurī, *Ansāb al-Ashrāf,* Vol. 1 (Cairo, Dār al-Ma'ārif, 1959), p. 270.

46. For details, see Musṭafā al-Zarqā', *Aḥkām al-Waqf,* Vol. 1 (Maṭba'at al-Jāmi'ah al-Sūrīyah, 1947), pp. 7–11.

47. For legal rules relating to *waqf* as well as for some historical details see Muḥammad Muḥammad Amīn, *al-Awqāf Wa'l-Ḥayāt al-Ijtimā'īyah fī Miṣr* (Cairo, Dār al-Nahḍah al-'Arabīyah, 1980); Muḥammad al-Ḥabīb al-Tajkānī, *Niẓām al-Tabarru'āt fī'l-Sharī'ah al-Islāmīyah* (Casablanca, Dār al-Nashr al-Maghribiyah, 1983); al-Khaṭīb al-'Umarī, *Mishkāt al-Maṣābīḥ*; Muḥammad 'Ubayd 'Abdullāh al-Kubaisis, *Aḥkām al-Waqf fī'l-Sharī'ah al-Islāmīyah,* 2 vols. (Baghdād, Maṭba'at al-Irshād, 1977).

48. It may be noted, however, that family endowments also have a clause rendering them into a charity in case none of the descendants survive (al-Kubaisis, *op. cit.*, Vol. 1, p. 43).

49. Al-Zarqā', *op. cit.*, p. 49.

50. Al-Kubaisis, *op. cit.*, Vol. 1, p. 45; Amīn, *op. cit.*, pp. 276–320.

51. Al-Kubaisis, *op. cit.*, Vol. 1, pp. 47–50.

52. For details see Muḥammad Nejatullah Siddiqi, 'Islamic Banking: Theory and Practice' in *Islam and the Economic Development of Southeast Asia: Islamic Banking in Southeast Asia,* ed. Mohamed Ariff (Singapore, Institute of Southeast Asian Studies, 1988), pp. 34–66.

Bibliography

Abdullah Yusuf Ali, *The Glorious Qur'ān, Translation and Commentary* (Leicester, The Islamic Foundation, 1978).

Abdun Noor, *Education and Basic Human Needs* (World Bank Staff Working Paper No. 450, 1981), p. 2.

Abū 'Awānah, *Musnad* (Hyderabad, Dā'irat al-Ma'ārif, 1362 AH).

Abū Dāwūd, *Sunan.*

Abū Fāris, Muḥammad 'Abd al-Qādir, *Infāq al-Zakāt fi' l-Maṣāliḥ al-'Āmmah* ('Ammān, Dār al-Furqān, 1983).

Abū 'Ubayd al-Qāsim bin Sallām, *Kitāb al-Amwāl* (Beirut, Dār al-Fikr, 1975).

Abū Ya'lā, *al-Aḥkām al-Sulṭānīyah* (Beirut, Dār al-Fikr, 1974).

Abū Yūsuf, *Kitāb al-Kharāj* (Cairo, al-Maṭba'ah al-Salafīyah, 1397 AH).

Abū Zahrah, Muḥammad, *Tanẓīm al-Islām li' l-Mujtama'* (Cairo, Dār al-Fikr al-'Arabī, 1975), p. 146.

Aḥmad bin Ḥanbal, *Musnad* (Beirut, al-Maktab al-Islāmī, n.d.).

Al-'Alī, Ṣāliḥ Aḥmad, *al-Tanẓīmāt al-Ijtimā'īyah wa' l-Iqtiṣādīyah fi' l-Baṣrah fī' l-Qarn al-Awwal al-Hijrī* (Beirut, Dār al-Ṭalī'ah, 1969).

Aliber, Robert Z., *The International Money Game* (Basic Books, 1987).

'Alī Haydar, *Durar al-Ḥukkām Sharḥ Majallat al-Aḥkām* (Beirut, n.d.).

'Alī al-Muttaqī, *Kanz al-'Ummāl,* Vol. 3 (Hyderabad, 1312 AH).

Al-Āmidī, Saifuddīn, *al-Aḥkām fī Uṣūl al-Aḥkām* (Beirut, Dār al-Kutub al-'Ilmiyah, 1980).

Amīn, Muḥammad Muḥammad, *al-Awqāf Wa' l-Ḥayāt al-Ijtimā'īyah fī Miṣr* (Cairo, Dār al-Nahdhah al-'Arabiyah, 1980).

Asad, Muhammad, *The Message of the Qur'ān* (London, E.J. Brill, 1980).

Al-Aṣbahānī, Abū al-Faraj, *Kitāb al-Aghānī* (Beirut, Mu'assasat Jamāl, n.d.).

Al-'Asqalānī, Ibn Ḥajar, *Fatḥ al-Bārī Sharḥ Ṣaḥīḥ al-Bukhārī* (Beirut, n.d.).

Al-Baghdādī, Ibn Ṭāhir, 'Abd al-Qāhir, *Kitāb Uṣūl al-Dīn* (Beirut, Dār al-Kutub al-Ummīyah, 1981).

Al-Balādhurī, Aḥmad bin Yaḥyā bin Jābir, *Futūḥ al-Buldān* (Cairo, Maṭba'at al-Mawsū'āt, 1932).

——, *Ansāb al-Ashrāf* (Cairo, Dār al-Ma'ārif, 1959).

Balassa, Bela, and Richard Nelson (eds.), *Economic Progress, Private Values and Public Policy: Essays in Honour of William Fellner* (Amsterdam, 1977).

Bāqir al-Ṣadr, Muḥammad, *Iqtiṣādunā* (Beirut, Dār al-Ta'āruf li'l-Maṭbū'āt, 1980).

Al-Bayhaqī, *al-Sunan al-Kubrā* (Beirut, Dār al-Fikr, n.d.).

Boulding, K.E., 'Allocation and Distribution: The Quarrelsome Twins' in *Value Judgement and Income Distribution,* ed. Robert A. Solo and Charles A. Anderson (Praeger, 1981).

Al-Bukhārī, Muḥammad bin Ismā'īl, *al-Jāmi' al-Ṣaḥīḥ.*

——, *al-Adab al-Mufrad* (Beirut, Dār Maktabat al-Ḥayāt, 1980).

Central Zakat Administration, *The Zakat Manual* (Islamabad, Ministry of Finance, 1982).

Chenery, Hollis et al., *Redistribution with Growth* (Oxford University Press, 1975).

Collard, David, *Altruism and Economy: A Study in Non-Selfish Behaviour* (Oxford, Martin Robertson, 1978).

Cooper, R.N., *The Gold Standard: Historical Facts and Future Prospects* (Brookings Institution Paper No. 1, 1982).

——, *Economic Policy in an Interdependent World* (Cambridge, Mass., 1986).

Al-Dihlawī, Shāh Walīullah, *Ḥujjatullāh al-Bālighah* (Beirut, Dār al-Ma'rifah, n.d.).

Danziger, Sheldon, 'How Income Transfers Affect Work, and the Income Distribution' in Robert Haveman and Robert Potnick, *Journal of Economic Literature,* Vol. xix, No. 3, pp. 975–1028.

Al-Darāquṭnī, 'Alī bin 'Umar, *Sunan* (Cairo, Dār al-Maḥāsin, n.d.).

Davidson, Paul, *International Money and the Real World* (New York, John Wiley & Sons, 1982).

Al-Dūrī, 'Abd al-'Azīz, *Ta'rīkh al-'Irāq al-Iqtiṣādī fī'l-Qarn al-Rābi' al-Hijrī* (Beirut, Dār al-Mashriq, 1974).

Elkan, Peter G., *The New Model Economy* (New York, Pergamon Press, 1982).

Fischel, Walter, J., *Jews in the Economic and Political Life of Medieval Islam* (London, Royal Asiatic Society, 1968).

——, 'The Origin of Banking in Medieval Islam', *JRAS* (1933), pp. 339–52.

Al-Ghazālī, Abū Ḥāmid, *al-Tibr al-Masbūk fī Naṣīḥat al-Mulūk* (Egypt, Maktabat al-Jundī, 1967).

——, *al-Mustasfā min 'Ilm al-Uṣūl* (Bulaq al-Maṭba'ah al-Amīrīyah, 1322 AH).

Al-Ghazālī, Muḥammad, *al-Islām wa'l-Manāhij al-Ishtirākīyah* (Cairo, 1951).

Goitein, S.D., *Studies in Islamic History and Institutions* (Leiden, E.J. Brill, 1968).

Grilli, Enzo R. and Maw Chung Yang: 'Primary Commodity Prices and the Terms of Trade of Developing Countries: What the Long Run Shows', *The World Bank Economic Review,* Vol. 2, No. 1 (Jan. 1988), pp. 1–47.

Al-Ḥākim, *al-Mustadrak,* Vol. 2 (Hyderabad, 1340 AH) and Aḥmad bin Ḥanbal, *Musnad,* narrations from Ibn 'Umar (ed. A.M. Shākir).

Al-Hamadhānī, Muḥammad bin 'Abd al-Malik, *Takmilat Ta'rīkh al-Ṭabarī,* in al-Ṭabarī, *Ta'rīkh,* Vol. 11 (Beirut, Dār Suwaydān, n.d.).

Ḥasan Ibrāhīm Ḥasan, *Ta'rīkh al-Islām,* Vol. III (Cairo, 1965).

Hasan-uz-Zaman, S.M., *The Economic Functions of the Early Islamic State* (Karachi: International Islamic Publishers, 1981).

Holt, P.M. et al. (eds.), *Cambridge History of Islam,* Vol. 1 (Cambridge, 1970).

Ibn 'Ābidīn, *Ḥāshiyat Radd al-Muḥtār* (Cairo, al-Maṭba'ah al-Maymanīyah, 1318 AH).

Ibn 'Abd al-Barr, *al-Istī'āb fī Ma'rifat al-Ṣaḥābah,* Vol. 1 (Hyderabad, 1318 AH).

Ibn 'Abd al-Ḥakam, *Sīrat 'Umar bin 'Abd al-'Azīz* (Egypt, al-Maṭba'ah al-Raḥmānīyah, 1927).

Ibn Amīr al-Ḥājj, Muḥammad, *al-Taqrīr wa'l-Taḥbīr (Sharḥ Kitāb al-Taḥrīr)* (Bulāq, 1316 AH).

Ibn al-Athīr, *al-Kāmil fi'l-Ta'rīkh* (Beirut, Dār al-Fikr, 1978).

Ibn Ḥabīb, Awb Ja'far Muḥammad, *Kitāb al-Muḥabbar* (Beirut, al-Maktabah al-Tijārī, n.d.).

Ibn Ḥazm, *al-Muḥallā,* Vol. 6 (Egypt, Maṭba'ah al-Nahḍah, 1347 AH).

Ibn Hishām, *Sīrat al-Nabī* (Beirut, Dār al-Fikr, n.d.).

Ibn al-Jawzī, *Sīrat 'Umar bin al-Khaṭṭāb* (Egypt, Maṭba'at al-Sa'ādah, 1924).

Ibn Kathīr, Ismā'īl bin 'Umar, *al-Bidāyah wa'l-Nihāyah* (Cairo, Maṭba'at al-Sa'ādah, 1935).

Ibn Khaldūn, *al-Muqaddimah* (Beirut, Dār al-Kutub al-Lubnānī, 1982).

Ibn Khallikān, *Wafayāt al-A'yān,* Vol. 6 (Cairo, Maktabat al-Nahḍah, 1948).

Ibn Mājah, *Sunan.*

Ibn Manẓūr, *Mukhtaṣar Tā'rīkh Dimashq li-Ibn 'Asākir,* Vol. 9 (Dimashq, Dār al-Fikr, 1985).

Ibn Sa'd, Muḥammad, *al-Ṭabaqāt al-Kubrā* (Beirut, Dār Ṣādir, n.d.).

Ibn Taymȳah, *al-Siyāsah al-Shar'īyah fī Aḥwāl al-Rā'ī wa'l-Ra'īyah* (Beirut, Dār al-Ma'rifah, 1969).

——, *Majmū' Fatāwā Shaykh al-Islām Aḥmad Ibn Taymīyah,* Vol. 29 (Riyāḍ, Al-Riyāḍ Press, 1383 AH).

——, *al-Ḥisbah fi'l-Islām* (Kuwait, Maktabat Dār al-Arqam, 1983).

Ibn al-Ṭiqṭaqā, *al-Fakhrī fi'l-Ādāb al-Sulṭānīyah* (Cairo, Maṭba'at al-Ma'ārif, 1923).

Ibrāhīm, Aḥmad Ibrāhīm, *Niẓām al-Nafaqāt fi'l-Sharī'at al-Islāmīyah* (1349 AH).

Imām al-Ḥaramayn al-Juwaynī, ʻAbd al-Malik bin ʻAbd Allāh, *Ghiyāth al-Umam fī Iltiyāth al-Ẓulam* (Cairo, Maṭbaʻat Nahḍat Miṣr, 1401 AH).

ʻIzzuddīn bin ʻAbd al-Salām, *Qawāʻid al-Aḥkām fī Maṣāliḥ al-Anām,* Vol. 1 (Egypt, al-Maṭbaʻah al-Ḥusaynīyah, 1934).

Al-Jaḥshiyarī, Abū ʻAbdullāh Muḥammed bin ʻAbdūs, *Kitāb al-Wuzarā' wa'l-Kuttāb* (Cairo, Muṣṭafā al-Bābī, 1980).

Al-Jaṣṣāṣ, Abū Bakr A., *Aḥkām al-Qur'ān,* Vol. 3 (al-Maṭbaʻah al-Salafiyah, 1395 AH).

Al-Jazīrī, ʻAbd al-Raḥmān, *Kitāb al-Fiqh ʻalā al-Madhāhib al-Arbaʻah* (Egypt, Sharikat Fann al-Ṭibāʻah, n.d.).

Johnson, Harry G., *International Trade and Economic Growth* (Cambridge, Mass., 1967).

Al-Kāsānī, Abū Bakr bin Masʻūd, *Badā'iʻ al-Ṣanā'iʻ fī Tartīb al-Sharā'iʻ* (Egypt, al-Maṭbaʻah al-Jamālīyah, 1910).

Al-Kattānī, ʻAbd al-Ḥayy bin ʻAbd al-Kabīr, *Niẓām al-Ḥukūmah al-Nabawīyah al-Musammā al-Tarātīb al-Idārīyah* (Beirut, Dār al-Kutub al-ʻArabī, n.d.).

Keynes, J.M., *The Collected Works of John Maynard Keynes,* Vol. XXV (Cambridge University Press, 1980).

Khadduri, Majid, *The Islamic Law of Nations, Shaybānī's Siyar* (Baltimore, Maryland, Johns Hopkins University Press, 1966).

Al-Khaṭīb, Aḥmad ʻAlī, *al-Waqf wa'l-Waṣāyā* (Baghdad, Maṭbaʻat Jāmiʻah Baghdād, 1978).

Al-Khaṭīb, al-ʻUmarī, *Mishkāt al-Maṣābīḥ.*

Al-Khuḍrī Beck, Muḥammad, *Muḥāḍarāt Ta'rīkh al-Umam al-Islāmīyah* (Beirut, Dār al-Qalam, 1986).

Al-Khuzāʻī, ʻAlī bin Muḥammad bin Saʻūd, *Takhrīj al-Dalālāt al-Samʻīyah ʻAlā mā Kāna fī ʻAhd Rasūl Allah . . .* (Beirut, Dār al-Gharb al-Islāmī, 1985).

Kindleberger, C.P., *International Economics* (Homewood, Ill, Richard D. Irwin Inc., 1968).

Krugman, Paul R., 'Is Free Trade Passe?', *Economic Perspectives,* Vol. 1, No. 2 (Fall 1987), pp. 131–44.

Al-Kubaisis, Muḥammad ʻUbayd ʻAbdullāh, *Aḥkām al-Waqf fī'l-Sharīʻah al-Islāmīyah,* 2 vols. (Baghdad, Maṭbaʻah al-Irshād, 1977).

Lutz, Mark A. and Kenneth Lux, *The Challenge of Humanistic Economics* (Menlo Park, California, Benjamin/Cummings Publishing Company, 1979).

McKenzie, Richard B. and Gordon Tullock, *The World of Economics: Explorations into Human Experience* (London, Richard D. Irwin Inc. 1975).

Mālik bin Anas, *al-Muwaṭṭa'*.

Al-Maqrīzī, *Kitāb al-Khiṭaṭ* (Lebanon, Maktabat Iḥyā' al-'Ulūm, n.d.).

Marmor, Theodore R. (ed.), *Poverty Policy – A Compendium of Cash Transfer Proposals* (Chicago, Aldine Atherton Inc., 1971).

Al-Mas'ūdī, *Murūj al-Dhahab* (Beirut, Dār al-Andalus, n.d.).

Al-Māwardī, 'Alī bin Muḥammad, *al-Aḥkām al-Sulṭāniyah* (Beirut, Dār al-Fikr, 1974).

——, *Kitāb Ādāb al-Dunyā wa'l-Dīn* (Beirut, Dār Iḥyā' al-Turāth al-'Arabī, 1979).

Al-Mawdūdī, Sayyid Abū'l A'lā, *Fatāwā al-Zakāh,* trans. Rafīq al-Miṣrī (Jeddah, Centre for Research in Islamic Economics, 1985).

——, *Ma'āshiyāt-e-Islām* (Lahore, Islamic Publications, 1969).

Metz, Adam, *al-Ḥaḍārah al-Islāmīyah fi'l-Qarn al-Rābi' al-Hijrī* (Beirut, Dār al-Kitāb al-'Arabī, 1967).

Miskawayh, Abū 'Alī Aḥmad, *Kitāb Tajārib al-Umam* (Baghdad, Maktabat al-Muthannā, 1914).

Al-Miṣrī, Rafīq, *Kitāb al-Zakāh.* Translation of *The Zakat Manual* issued by the Central Zakat Administration, Pakistan, with an introduction (Jeddah, Centre for Research in Islamic Economics, 1984).

Al-Mubārak, Muḥammad, *Niẓām al-Islām: al-Iqtiṣād* (Beirut, Dār al-Fikr, 1980).

Al-Mubarrad, Abū al-'Abbās, *al-Kāmil* (Cairo, Musṭafā al-Bābī, 1936).

Muḥammad bin Aḥmad, *Ta'rīkh Miṣr,* Vol. 1 (Bulāq, 1311 AH).

Musgrave, Richard A. and Musgrave, Peggy B., *Public Finance in Theory and Practice* (McGraw Hill, 1984).

Muslim, *Ṣaḥīḥ* (Cairo, Dār al-Sha'b, n.d.).

Al-Nasā'ī, *Sunan.*

Al-Nawawī, *Minhāj al-Ṭālibīn wa 'Umdat al-Muftīn* (Cairo, Dār Iḥyā' al-Kutub al-'Arabī, 1318 AH).

Okun, Arthur M., *The Big Trade Off* (Washington DC, The Brookings Institution, 1975).

Perlman, Richard, *The Economics of Poverty* (McGraw Hill, 1976).

Phelps, Edmund S. (ed.), *Private Wants and Public Needs* (New York, W.W. Norton & Company, 1965).

Pickthall, M.M., *The Glorious Qur'ān* (Makkah, The Muslim World League, 1977).

Al-Qalaqashandī, Abū' 'Abbās Aḥmad bin 'Alī, *Subḥ al-A'shā* (Cairo, n.d.).

Al-Qaraḍāwī, Yūsuf, *Fiqh al-Zakāt* (Beirut, 1981).

Al-Qurṭubī, Abū 'Abdullāh, *al-Jāmi' li-Aḥkām al-Qur'ān* (Cairo, Dār al-Kutub al-Miṣrīyah, 1952).

Al-Qurṭubī, Arīb bin Sa'd, *Ṣilat Ta'rīkh al-Ṭabarī* in al-Ṭabarī, *Ta'rīkh,* Vol. II (Beirut, Dār Suwaydān, n.d.).

Quṭb, Sayyid, *al-'Adālah al-ijtimā'īyah fī'l-Islām* (Beirut, 1967).

Al-Ramlī, Shihābuddīn Aḥmad, *Nihāyat al-Muḥtāj ilā Sharḥ al-Minhāj,* Vol. 6 (Egypt, n.d.).

Raquibuzzaman, M., *Some Administrative Aspects of Collection and Disbursement of Zakah* (Jeddah, Centre for Research in Islamic Economics, 1987).

Rushton, J. Philippe and Richard M. Sorrentino (eds.), *Altruism and Helping Behaviour: Personality and Development Perspective* (Hellsdale, New Jersey, Lawrence Elbaum Associates, 1981).

Al-Ṣābi', Abū al-Ḥasan al-Hilāl b. al-Muḥassin, *al-Wuzarā'* (Cairo, Dār Iḥyā' al-Kutub al-'Arabīyah, 1958).

Al-Ṣamhūdī, Nūr al-dīn 'Alī bin Aḥmad, *Wafā' al-Wafā' bi-Akhbār Dār al-Muṣṭafā* (Beirut, Dār Iḥyā' al-Turāth al-'Arabī, 1971).

Samuelson, Paul A., *The Collective Scientific Papers of Paul A. Samuelson,* ed. Joseph E. Stiglitz (Oxford & IBH Publishing Co., 1966).

Al-Sarakhsī, Shams al-dīn, *Kitāb al-Mabsūṭ,* 3rd Print (Beirut, Dār al-Ma'rifah, n.d.).

Sarakhsī: *Sharḥ Kitāb al-siyar al-Kabīr li-Muḥammad bin Ḥasan al-Shaybānī,* ed. Salāḥ al-dīn al-Munajjid (Cairo, 1971).

Shahabuddin, Syed (ed.), *Muslim India,* Vol. IV, No. 40 (April 1986).

Al-Shāṭibī, Abū Isḥāq, *Al-Muwāfaqāt fī Uṣūl al-Sharī'ah* (Cairo, al-Maktabah al-Tijārīyah, n.d.).

Al-Shaybānī, Muḥammad bin al-Ḥasan, *Kitāb al-Āthār.*

Siddiqi, Muhammad Nejatullah, *Islām kā Nazarīyah-e-Milkīyat* (Lahore, 1968; Delhi, 1978).

——, *Banking Without Interest* (Leicester, The Islamic Foundation, 1983).

——, 'Islamic Banking: Theory and Practice' in *Islam and the Economic Development of South East Asia: Islamic Banking in South East Asia,* ed. Mohamed Ariff (Singapore, Institute of South East Asian Studies, 1988).

Singer, Hans, *Technologies for Basic Needs* (Geneva, ILO, 1977), p. 104.

Singer, Peker, 'Freedom and Utilities in the Distribution of Health Care' in *Market and Morals,* ed. Gerald Dovorkin, Gordon Bermant and Peter G. Brown (Washington, Hampshire Publishing Company, 1977).

Spraos, John, *Inequalizing Trade, A Study of Trade of Traditional North-South Specialization in the Context of the Terms of Trade Concepts* (Oxford, 1983).

Streeten, Paul P., *Basic Needs: Some Issues,* World Bank and Shahid Javed Burki: Reprint series 53. Reprinted from *World Development* 6 (1978).

——, 'Basic Needs: Premises and Promises' in *Journal of Policy Modelling,* Vol. 1 (1979), pp. 136–46.

——, 'From Growth to Basic Needs' in *Poverty and Basic Needs* (The World Bank, Sept. 1980), p. 8.

Al-Ṣūlī, Abū Bakr Muḥammad b. Yaḥyā, *Akhbār al-Rāḍī wa'l-Muttaqī min Kitāb al-Awrāq* (Beirut, Dār al-Masīrah, 1979).

——, *Ādāb al-Kuttāb* (Beirut, Dār al-Bāz li'l-Ṭibā'ah wa'l-Nashr, n.d.).

Al-Ṭabarānī, *Al-Mu'jam al-Ṣaghīr* (Delhi, Maṭba'ah Anṣar, 1311 AH).

Al-Ṭabarī, *Ta'rīkh* (Beirut, Dār Suwaydān, n.d.).

Al-Tajkānī, Muḥammad al-Ḥabīb, *Niẓām al-Tabarru'āt fi' l-Sharī'ah al-Islāmīyah* (Casablanca, Dār al-Nashr al-Maghribīyah, 1983).

Al-Tanūkhī, al-Qāḍī Abū 'Alī al-Muḥsin b. 'Alī, *Nishwār al-Muḥāḍarah wa Akhbār al-Mudhākarah,* 8 Vols. (Beirut, Sharikat al-Fajr al-'Arabī, 1971).

Al-Tirmidhī, *Sunan.*

Tussing, A. Dale, *Poverty in a Dual Economy* (New York, St. Martin's Press, 1975).

Tyser, C.R., *The Majelle* (Lahore, Law Publishing Company, 1980).

Udovitch, A.L., 'Reflections on the Institution of Credit and Banking in the Medieval Islamic Near East', *Studia Islamica,* Vol. 41 (1975), pp. 5–21.

Al-Wakī', Muḥammad bin Khalaf bin Ḥayyān, Akhbār al-Quḍāt (Beirut, 'Ālam al-Kutub, n.d.).

Weitzman, Martin L., *The Share Economy* (Cambridge, Mass., Harvard University Press, 1984).

Williams, Frances (ed.), *Why the Poor Pay More* (London, Macmillan, 1977).

Yaḥyā bin Ādam, *Kitāb al-Kharāj* (Cairo, al-Maṭba'ah al-Salafiyah, 1347 AH).

Yūsuf, Ibrāhīm Yūsuf, *al-Nafaqāt al-'Āmmah fi' l-Islām; Dirāsah Muqārinah* (Cairo, Dār al-Kutub al-Jāmi'ī, 1980).

Al-Zarkashī, Muḥammad bin Bahādur, *al-Manthūr fi' l-Qawā'id* (Kuwait, Ministry of Awqaf, 1982).

Al-Zarqa, Muhammad Anas, 'Islamic Distributive Schemes' in *Distributive Justice and Need Fulfilment in an Islamic Economy,* ed. Munawar Iqbal (Islamabad, International Institute of Islamic Economics, 1986).

Al-Zarqā', Muṣṭafā, *Aḥkām al-Waqf,* 1 (Maṭba'at al-Jāmi'ah al-Sūrīyah, 1947).

Index